# GCSE OCR 21ˢᵗ Century
# *Biology*
## The Workbook

This book is for anyone doing **GCSE OCR 21ˢᵗ Century Biology**.

It's full of **tricky questions**... each one designed to make you **sweat**
— because that's the only way you'll get any **better**.

There are questions to see **what facts** you know. There are questions
to see how well you can **apply those facts**. And there are questions
to see what you know about **how science works**.

It's also got some daft bits in to try and make the whole
experience at least vaguely entertaining for you.

## *What CGP is all about*

Our sole aim here at CGP is to produce the highest
quality books — carefully written, immaculately presented
and dangerously close to being funny.

Then we work our socks off to get them
out to you — at the cheapest possible prices.

# Contents

## MODULE B5 — GROWTH AND DEVELOPMENT

## MODULE B6 — BRAIN AND MIND

## MODULE B7 — FURTHER BIOLOGY

Published by CGP

Editors:
Joe Brazier, Emma Elder, Murray Hamilton, Edmund Robinson, Hayley Thompson.

Contributors:
Jane Davies, Paddy Gannon, Dr Iona MJ Hamilton, Claire Ruthven, Adrian Schmit.

ISBN: 978 1 84762 613 4

With thanks to Charlotte Burrows, Janet Cruse-Sawyer, Ben Fletcher, Sue Hocking and Julie Jackson for the proofreading.

With thanks to Laura Jakubowski for the copyright research.

Groovy website: www.cgpbooks.co.uk

Printed by Elanders Ltd, Newcastle upon Tyne.
Jolly bits of clipart from CorelDRAW®

Based on the classic CGP style created by Richard Parsons.

# Module B1 — You and Your Genes

## Genes, Chromosomes and DNA

**Q1** Tick the boxes to show whether the following statements are **true** or **false**.

|  |  | True | False |
|---|---|---|---|
| a) | The nucleus of a cell contains instructions for how an organism develops. | ☐ | ☐ |
| b) | Genes are short lengths of chromosomes. | ☐ | ☐ |
| c) | DNA is made up of chromosomes. | ☐ | ☐ |
| d) | There are 23 pairs of genes. | ☐ | ☐ |
| e) | Genes are instructions for a cell that describe how to make proteins. | ☐ | ☐ |

**Q2** **Proteins** are either **structural** or **functional**.

a) Give **one** example of a structural protein.

.............................................................................................................................

b) Give **one** example of a functional protein.

.............................................................................................................................

**Q3** Complete these sentences by circling the correct word(s) from each pair.

Some characteristics (e.g. scars) are controlled only by an organism's **environment / genes**.

Other traits, like dimples, are controlled by the organism's **environment / genes**.

Weight is a characteristic that's controlled by an organism's **genes alone / genes and environment**.

Many genetic traits, like eye colour, rely on **just one gene / several genes working together**.

**Q4** Describe the difference between an organism's **genotype** and its **phenotype**.

.............................................................................................................................

.............................................................................................................................

.............................................................................................................................

**Top Tips:** Remember, human body cells have **23 pairs** of chromosomes (that's 46 in total). Chromosomes carry genes that provide instructions for cells about how to make different proteins — the different proteins that are responsible for all of your genetic traits. Biology never ceases to amaze...

# Genes and Variation

**Q1**    The diagram below shows two cells from the same organism.

**Add labels** to the diagram to show which cell is a **sex cell** and which is a **body cell**.

a)..........................................

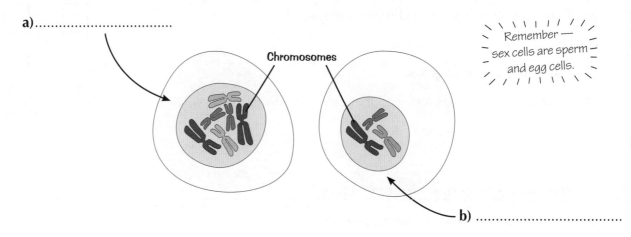

Chromosomes

*Remember — sex cells are sperm and egg cells.*

b) ..................................

**Q2**    There are **46 chromosomes** in a human body cell.

a)   How many chromosomes would you find in a human **skin** cell? ..................................................

b)   How many chromosomes would you find in a human **sex** cell? ..................................................

c)   How many **copies** of each chromosome would you find in a **sex** cell? ..........................................

d)   How many **copies** of each chromosome would you find in a **skin** cell? ..........................................

**Q3**    Complete the passage using some of the words given below.

| all | exactly | cells | chromosomes |
|-----|---------|-------|-------------|
| gene | a bit | parent | some |

Half of a child's ................................... have come from each ................................... .

This means that children will look ................................... like both of them, but won't

be ................................... like either one because ................................... of the alleles

came from the other parent.

___

**_Top Tips:_**    All of this is pretty mind-boggling stuff.  It's weird to think you only look the way you do because of lots of random events that took place when you were being created.  You can blame your dad for your weedy wrists and your mum for your knobbly knees, but you've only got yourself to blame for that dodgy haircut — oh well, at least it'll grow back...

# Genes and Variation

**Q4** The diagram shows a **pair** of human **chromosomes**. These chromosomes carry a **gene** for **ear lobes**. The position of the gene is marked on one of the chromosomes in the diagram.

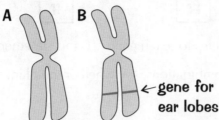
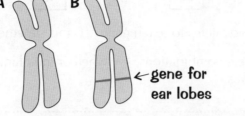

← gene for ear lobes

**a)** Draw the position of the gene for ear lobes on chromosome A.

**b)** If chromosome A came from the **mother** where must chromosome B have come from?

..................................................................................................................

**c)** What are **alleles**?

..................................................................................................................

**d)** Chromosome A contains a **different allele** of the ear lobe gene from chromosome B. Underline the correct statement below.

Sex cells contain the instructions for both versions of ear lobe.

Sex cells will only contain the instructions for one version of ear lobe.

**Q5** The picture below shows two **sisters**. They have the **same parents** but don't bear a close resemblance to one another.

Complete the following statements by circling the correct word(s) to explain why two sisters (or brothers) can look quite different from each other, even though they have the same parents.

Despite inheriting **all / none / half** of their genes from the same mother and **all / none / half** from the same father, siblings don't look identical. This is because of the way **sex cells / liver cells** are made and the way they **combine / separate**. There are **tens / millions** of different combinations.

Every person in the world will have **a unique / the same** combination of alleles — that's why no two people in the world are exactly the same, with the exception of **cousins / identical twins**.

**4**

# Inheritance and Genetic Diagrams

**Q1**  A species of plant has **two alleles** for **flower colour**. The allele for **violet** flowers **(F)** is **dominant** over the allele for **white** flowers **(f)**. The possible allele combinations are shown below.

| FF | Ff | ff |

a) "Individuals usually have two alleles for each gene." Is this statement **true** or **false**? ......................

b) For each of the different allele combinations, say whether the plant is **homozygous** or **heterozygous**.

   i) FF ...................................................................................................................................

   ii) Ff ...................................................................................................................................

   iii) ff ...................................................................................................................................

c) What **colour** flowers would the plants with these alleles have? Circle the correct answer.

   i) FF                 **violet / white**

   ii) Ff                 **violet / white**

   iii) ff                 **violet / white**

*I think it should be violet*

*Violet it is.*

**Q2**  In cats, the allele for black fur **(B)** is **dominant** over the allele for brown fur **(b)**. Two black cats, Jasper and Belle, have a litter of kittens. Most are black, but one is brown. Tick the boxes to show whether the following statements are **true** or **false**.

                                                         **True**    **False**

a) The brown kitten has the alleles bb.     ☐    ☐

b) Jasper's alleles are BB.     ☐    ☐

c) Belle's alleles could be Bb or bb.     ☐    ☐

d) The brown kitten must be a mutation — all the kittens should be black.     ☐    ☐

*It might be easier to answer the questions if you draw a genetic diagram.*

**Q3**  Some people can roll their tongue and others can't. The ability to tongue roll is controlled by a single gene. **Rolling (R)** is **dominant** to **non-rolling (r)**.

Izzy can roll her tongue but Saaj cannot. What conclusions can you draw about Izzy and Saaj's genetic make-up for the tongue rolling gene? Explain your answer.

...................................................................................................................................................

...................................................................................................................................................

...................................................................................................................................................

# Inheritance and Genetic Diagrams

**Q4**  The **family tree** below shows a family with a gene for x-ray vision. The **normal** vision allele (**N**) is **dominant** over the allele for **x-ray** vision (**n**).

a)  Based on the expression of this gene, write the combination of **alleles** each grandchild has.

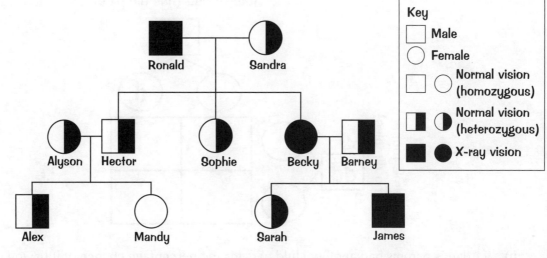

Key
- Male
- Female
- Normal vision (homozygous)
- Normal vision (heterozygous)
- X-ray vision

Alleles:  ...................   ...................   ...................   ...................

b)  **Hector** and **Alyson** are expecting another baby. What is the chance that the new baby will have **x-ray** vision? Give your answer as a **percentage**.

......................................................................................................................................

c)  Hector thinks that the baby will **definitely** have **x-ray** vision because Alex and Mandy don't. Is Hector right? Explain your answer.

......................................................................................................................................

......................................................................................................................................

**Q5**  In **guinea pigs**, the allele for short hair (**H**) is dominant over the allele for long hair (**h**).

a)  Is it possible for two short haired guinea pigs to produce long haired offspring? Explain your answer.

......................................................................................................................................

......................................................................................................................................

b)  Is it possible for two long haired guinea pigs to produce short haired offspring? Explain your answer.

......................................................................................................................................

......................................................................................................................................

# Genetic Diagrams and Sex Chromosomes

**Q1**     In humans, the allele for cheeks with **dimples** (**D**) is **dominant** over the allele for cheeks with **no dimples** (**d**). Adam's mum has no dimples and his dad is **heterozygous** for the trait.

a)     Complete the Punnett square below to show the genetic cross between Adam's parents.

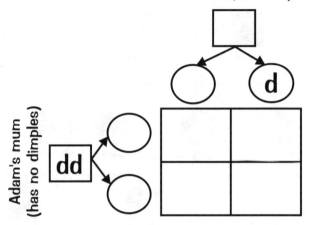

**Adam's dad (has dimples)**

Adam's mum (has no dimples)

dd

d

b)     If Adam's parents had another child, what is the **percentage chance** of it having dimples?

..............................................................................................................................................................................

**Q2**     Fill in the gaps in the passage below about how a person's **sex** is determined.

Everybody has one pair of chromosomes that determine whether they

are male or female. These chromosomes are called the ..........................

chromosomes. There are two types, the .......................... chromosome,

which can be found in males and females, and the ..........................

chromosome, which is found in .......................... only.

**Q3**     The sex of a developing human embryo is controlled by a **gene** that causes the production of a specific **protein**.

a)     Explain how the protein controls the sex of a developing embryo.

..............................................................................................................................................................................

..............................................................................................................................................................................

..............................................................................................................................................................................

b)     Which chromosome do you think the gene that codes for the protein is found on?

..............................................................................................................................................................................

# Genetic Disorders

**Q1** **Huntington's disease** is caused by a **faulty** allele of a single gene.

a) Is Huntington's disease caused by a dominant or recessive allele? ..................................................

b) It is possible for a person to pass the disorder on to their children unknowingly. Why is this?

..............................................................................................................................................

..............................................................................................................................................

c) Give three symptoms that someone suffering from Huntington's disease might display.

1. ........................................ 2. ........................................ 3. ........................................

**Q2** Libby and Anne are pregnant. They both have a history of **cystic fibrosis** in their families, but they don't know if their babies will have the disorder.

|  | Drew | Libby | | Billy | Anne |
|---|---|---|---|---|---|
| Parent's phenotype: | Carrier | Carrier | | Carrier | Normal |
| Parent's genotype: | Ff | Ff | | Ff | FF |
| Baby's genotype: | | ? | | | ? |

*Remember — alleles with capital letters are dominant. Alleles with a small letter are recessive.*

a) It is possible to have the allele for cystic fibrosis, yet not know it because you show no symptoms. How is this possible?

..............................................................................................................................................

..............................................................................................................................................

b) Give three symptoms that someone suffering from cystic fibrosis might display.

1. ........................................................................................................................................

2. ........................................................................................................................................

3. ........................................................................................................................................

c) Complete the table to show the **percentage chances** of Libby's and Anne's babies being carriers or sufferers of cystic fibrosis.

|  | Carrier | Sufferer |
|---|---|---|
| Libby | | |
| Anne | | |

*Sketch a genetic diagram if it helps.*

# Genetic Testing

**Q1** Rod and Jane are currently undergoing *in-vitro* fertilisation (IVF) treatment.
It involves **creating embryos** outside of the body by mixing egg and sperm cells.

a) The embryos are **tested** for genetic disorders before being implanted into the mother's womb.

    **i)** What name is given to this process?

    ......................................................................................................................................

    **ii)** Explain why this test might be carried out.

    ......................................................................................................................................

b) Genetic tests can also be carried out on fetuses in the womb.
Give **one risk** of sampling cells from the fetus for a genetic test.

......................................................................................................................................

**Q2** **Genetic testing** can also be used on adults.

a) Suggest **one** reason why adults might want to have a test for a **genetic disorder**.

......................................................................................................................................

b) Explain how genetic testing can help doctors to **prescribe drugs**.

......................................................................................................................................

......................................................................................................................................

c) Are genetic tests always **100% accurate**?
Explain your answer and describe a problem this might cause.

......................................................................................................................................

......................................................................................................................................

......................................................................................................................................

**Q3** Give an example of how genetic testing could lead to **discrimination**.

......................................................................................................................................

......................................................................................................................................

***Top Tips:***    Genetic testing brings up some important issues and questions. You definitely need to know all of this for your exam, but it's actually the sort of stuff that's good to know anyway — it's likely to become more and more important as medicine advances.

*Module B1 — You and Your Genes*

# Clones

**Q1** Tick the boxes to show whether the following statements are **true** or **false**.

True    False

a) Bacteria can reproduce by asexual reproduction.

b) Asexual reproduction involves two parents.

c) Asexual reproduction produces genetically varied offspring.

**Q2** Plants can reproduce **asexually**.

Give two ways in which they can do this.

1. ...................................................................................................................

2. ...................................................................................................................

**Q3** **Identical twins** are natural **clones**.

a) Explain how the way they are formed makes identical twins **genetically identical**.

.............................................................................................................

.............................................................................................................

b) If identical twins are genetically identical, what factors must be responsible for any differences between them?

.............................................................................................................

**Q4** Complete the passage using the words provided.
You may need to use some words more than once.

| nucleus | not | material | embryo | swimming | host |
|---|---|---|---|---|---|
| donor | dividing | cytoplasm | genetically | egg | |

Clones are ............................ identical organisms. Animal clones can be made

by scientists in the laboratory by removing the ............................ from an

............................ cell (leaving it without any genetic ............................ ).

It is replaced with a nucleus taken from an adult ............................ cell.

The cell is then stimulated to start ............................ . The embryo that results

from this is ............................ identical to the ............................ cell.

# *Stem Cells*

**Q1** Tick the boxes to show whether the following statements are true or false.   **True**   **False**

a) Most cells in your body are specialised to carry out a specific role.   ☐   ☐

b) Stem cells can be found in early embryos.   ☐   ☐

c) Most cells of multicellular organisms become specialised
during early development of the organism.   ☐   ☐

**Q2** Complete the passage below about **stem cells** by using the words below to fill in the gaps.

| adult | unspecialised | any type | baby | certain types | specialised |
|-------|---------------|----------|------|---------------|-------------|

Embryonic stem cells are ............................. and have

the potential to turn into ............................. of cell.

............................. stem cells are also unspecialised but they're

less versatile — they can only turn into ............................. of cell.

**Q3** Read the following article about **embryonic stem cells** and answer the questions below.

Scientists are using embryonic stem cells for research into the treatment of different illnesses.
The process of extracting stem cells from an embryo destroys it. This is seen by some people
as a waste of a potential life. However, some fertility clinics donate unwanted embryos to
research scientists. These donated embryos would be destroyed anyway, so some people
think it's better that they're used for research rather than nothing at all.

a) Dahlia **supports** embryonic stem cell research using **unwanted embryos**.
Pete is **totally against** embryonic stem cell research.
Using the article above, describe **one** reason for both Dahlia and Pete's opinions.

Dahlia: ...........................................................................................................................................

...........................................................................................................................................

Pete: ...........................................................................................................................................

...........................................................................................................................................

b) Suggest **one** way in which embryonic stem cells could be used to treat illnesses.

...........................................................................................................................................

...........................................................................................................................................

# Mixed Questions — Module B1

**Q1**  Put the following in **order of size**, starting with the biggest.

> nucleus    cell    gene    chromosome    organism

........................  ........................  ........................  ........................  ........................

**Q2**  The pictures below show the chromosomes of two people.  One is **male** and the other is **female**.

Person A

Person B

**a)**  Which person is **female**? ................................................................................................................

**b)**  How can you tell? ................................................................................................................

**Q3 a)**  A genetic disorder is caused by a **dominant** allele (**T**).  Draw a **Punnett square** in the space below showing a cross between two individuals who are both **heterozygous** for the allele **T**.

**b)  i)**  What is the percentage chance of having a child that's a **sufferer** of the disorder from the cross above?

........................................................................................................................................

**ii)**  What is the percentage chance of having a child that has at least one copy of the **recessive** allele from the cross above?

........................................................................................................................................

# Mixed Questions — Module B1

**Q4** A **genetic disease** is caused by a **recessive** allele (a). It causes **severe disability** in sufferers.

The diagram below shows a cross between Sean and Jenny, who are both carriers of the recessive allele. Jenny knows that she is a carrier but Sean is not yet aware that he is. Sean and Jenny have two children — neither child has the disease.

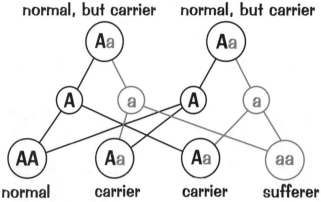

My son Jeremy shall inherit my stamp collection and my chromosomes.

**a)** What is the **percentage chance** that their third child will have the disease.

................................................................................................................................................

**b)** Sean has a genetic test and he finds out that he is a carrier of the disease.

**i)** Suggest **two** issues regarding his **family** that Sean may have to think about now he knows he is a carrier.

................................................................................................................................................

................................................................................................................................................

................................................................................................................................................

**ii)** Describe the implications of the use of the results of genetic tests by **insurance companies** and **employers**.

................................................................................................................................................

................................................................................................................................................

................................................................................................................................................

**c)** Jenny becomes pregnant again. A genetic test is carried out on the fetus and it's found to be **homozygous** for the **a allele**.

**i)** Is the fetus normal, a carrier or a sufferer of the disease?

................................................................................................................................................

**ii)** Suggest **one** issue regarding the **pregnancy** that Jenny and Sean may have to think about now they have the results of the genetic test.

................................................................................................................................................

# Microorganisms and Disease

**Q1** Complete the passage using the some of words provided below.

| bacteria | cats | directly | flowers | cells | viruses |
|----------|------|----------|---------|-------|---------|
| treats | symptoms | poisons | indirectly | feet | dogs |

Microorganisms are things like ................................. and ................................. .

Some microorganisms cause infectious diseases.  The effects that an infectious

disease has on the body are called ................................. . They are the result

of damage caused to the body's ................................. . This damage can be

caused ................................. by the microorganisms themselves or by

................................. produced by microorganisms.

**Q2** Jenny is growing a culture of the bacterium *Boringus dullus*.
At 30 °C the bacterium reproduces **once** every **15 minutes**.

**a)** If Jenny leaves **ten** *B. dullus* bacteria to reproduce for **two hours** at 30 °C,
how many bacteria will she have?

..................................................................................................................

..................................................................................................................

..................................................................................................................

..................................................................................................................

*You'll need to use a calculator to help you with this question.*

**b)** At 20 °C it takes a single *B. dullus* bacterium twice as long to reproduce.
If **one** bacterium was left at this temperature for **two hours**, how many bacteria will there be?

..................................................................................................................

..................................................................................................................

..................................................................................................................

**c)** Explain why bacteria can reproduce rapidly in the human body.

..................................................................................................................

..................................................................................................................

**Top Tips:**    There's one main thing to remember when you're working out the population
growth of some microorganisms — when enough time has passed for each one to reproduce, the total
number of microorganisms will have **doubled**.  It's pretty straightforward, but make sure you know this.

# The Immune System

**Q1**    What is the **role** of the immune system?

.......................................................................................................................................................

**Q2**    Some white blood cells can produce **antibodies** to deal with invading microorganisms.

**a)**    Can an antibody recognise a wide range of microorganisms?  Explain your answer.

.......................................................................................................................................................

.......................................................................................................................................................

**b)**    Describe another way that white blood cells can destroy microorganisms.

.......................................................................................................................................................

**Q3**    Underline the correct description of an **antigen**.          A 'foreign' cell.

A chemical that causes disease.        A molecule found on the        A molecule that destroys bacteria.
surface of a microorganism.

**Q4 a)**    Put the stages in order (1-4) to show how **white blood cells** deal with infection caused by a microorganism.

☐    The antibodies attach to the microorganism.

☐    White blood cells detect the surface antigens of the invading microorganism.

☐    An antibody that can attack the microorganism is produced.

☐    The microorganism is killed.

**b)**    Outline what would happen if the **same** microorganism was encountered again.
You should refer to **memory cells** in your answer.

.......................................................................................................................................................

.......................................................................................................................................................

**Q5**    Mike's little sister has **chicken pox**.  Mike had it himself when he was four.
He **doesn't think** he will catch it again.  Is he right?  Explain your answer.

.......................................................................................................................................................

.......................................................................................................................................................

.......................................................................................................................................................

# *Vaccination*

**Q1**  Vaccination usually involves injecting the body with a **dead** or **inactive** form of microorganism. State whether the following statements about polio immunisation are **true** or **false**.

**True  False**

a) The dead or inactive polio microorganisms still have antigens.  ☐ ☐

b) White blood cells produce antibodies to attack the injected polio microorganisms.  ☐ ☐

c) After the vaccination, white bloods cells can produce antibodies to fight typhoid.  ☐ ☐

d) The polio vaccine is completely safe for everyone.  ☐ ☐

**Q2 a)** Explain why the dead or inactive microorganisms in vaccinations cause the body to produce **antibodies**.

..................................................................................................................................

..................................................................................................................................

**b)** Explain how a vaccination provides **long-term protection** against a microorganism.

..................................................................................................................................

..................................................................................................................................

..................................................................................................................................

**Q3**  The MMR vaccine protects against **measles**, **mumps** and **rubella**.

a) Give **one** reason why vaccines aren't completely risk-free for everyone.

..................................................................................................................................

b) Why do people react differently to vaccines?

..................................................................................................................................

c) The Government recommends that **all** children are given the MMR vaccine. Explain why this is.

..................................................................................................................................

..................................................................................................................................

**Top Tips:**  Vaccination is a really effective way of controlling the spread of a disease and preventing big outbreaks of it (**epidemics**).  Just like revising is a really effective way of passing exams...

# *Antimicrobials*

**Q1** Explain the difference between an **antibody** and an **antimicrobial**.

..............................................................................................................................................................

..............................................................................................................................................................

**Q2** Jenny has a throat infection. Her doctor has told her that it's caused by a **virus**. Explain why he **didn't** give Jenny any antibiotics.

..............................................................................................................................................................

**Q3** In 1970, a **new antibiotic** was discovered which was very effective against **disease X**. Doctors have been prescribing this drug ever since. The graph below shows the number of deaths from disease X over a number of years.

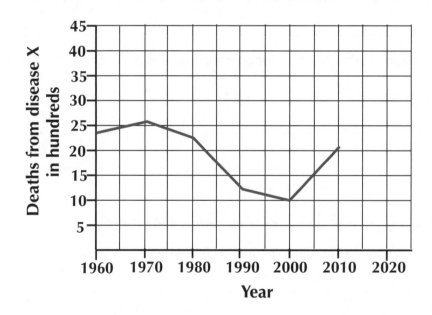

**a)** Using the graph, **calculate** how many more deaths from disease X there were in **1970** than in **2000**.

..............................................................................................................................................................

**b)** Assuming nothing changes, use the graph to **predict** the number of deaths from disease X in **2020**.

..............................................................................................................................................................

**c)** Suggest a reason for the **sudden rise** in deaths from the disease between 2000 and 2010.

..............................................................................................................................................................

..............................................................................................................................................................

# Antimicrobials

**Q4** There is concern about the appearance of **superbugs** (microorganisms that are resistant to most known antimicrobials).

a) Put the stages in order (1-4) to show how a population of microorganisms can develop **resistance** to a particular antimicrobial over a period of time.

☐ The mutated gene becomes more common in the population over time — giving the population resistance to the antimicrobial.

☐ The microorganism can survive and reproduce in a host being treated with the antimicrobial.

☐ A random mutation in the DNA of a microorganism means that it is less affected by the antimicrobial.

☐ The mutated gene for resistance will be passed on to the microorganism's offspring.

b) Doctors should **avoid prescribing antibiotics** for minor ailments if patients can do without them. Explain how this action reduces the chance of more superbugs appearing.

...................................................................................................................................

...................................................................................................................................

**Q5** The graph shows the number of bacteria in Gary's blood during a two-week course of **antibiotics**.

Symptoms are present when the level of bacteria is above this line.

a) How long after starting the course of antibiotics did Gary's symptoms disappear? .........................

b) Why is it important for Gary to finish his full course of antibiotics?

...................................................................................................................................

...................................................................................................................................

# Drug Trials

**Q1**    Before a drug can be sold, it is tested on a variety of different cells and organisms.  Put the cells and organisms in the order that drugs would be tested on.  The first one has been done for you.

| 1 | Human cells in a laboratory |

| | Sufferers of the disease |

| | Healthy human beings |

| | Mammals (other than humans) |

**Q2**    Explain why, during drug trials, the following are usually used to test drugs on:

a)  **Live mammals**.

..............................................................................................................................................

b)  **Human cells** grown in a lab.

..............................................................................................................................................

**Q3**    Before a drug is tested on sufferers, **clinical trials** are carried out with **healthy volunteers**.

a)  Explain why healthy people are used to test the drug before the sufferers.

..............................................................................................................................................

..............................................................................................................................................

b)  Explain why the drug will eventually need to be tested on sufferers as well.

..............................................................................................................................................

..............................................................................................................................................

c)  Some clinical trials can last for several months or even years.
     Give two reasons why it's important that human trials are long-term.

1. ..........................................................................................................................................

2. ..........................................................................................................................................

---

***Top Tips:***    Testing drugs on animals is a very controversial issue.  Some people think it's unethical and cruel to use animals in this way.  Currently the law states that drugs must be tested on animals before they can be used on humans.  A suitable alternative is needed before this can change.

# Drug Trials

**Q4**    An on-line advertisement for a new drug states that taking it can reduce 'bad' cholesterol by 52% (compared with 7% using a **placebo**) and increase 'good' cholesterol by 14% (compared with 3% using a placebo).

**a)**    What is a placebo?

...................................................................................................................................................

**b)**    In trialling this drug, suggest why the manufacturer used a placebo.

...................................................................................................................................................

**c)**    Suggest why a placebo might not be used if the drug being tested was a possible cure for advanced cancer.

...................................................................................................................................................

**Q5**    A new drug for a skin condition was being tested on patients that had the condition. The testers were using a **double-blind** trial. Some of the patients were given a cream containing the drug, while others were given a placebo. Neither the patients nor the scientists were told which batch of cream had the drug in it.

**a)**    Explain how a blind trial is different from a double-blind trial.

...................................................................................................................

...................................................................................................................

...................................................................................................................

**b)**    Why were the patients not told which cream they were given?

...................................................................................................................................................

...................................................................................................................................................

**c)**    Why were the scientists not told?

...................................................................................................................................................

...................................................................................................................................................

**d)**    If this drug is useful, suggest what results you would expect to see?

...................................................................................................................................................

...................................................................................................................................................

# The Circulatory System

**Q1**  Complete the passage using the words provided below.

| carbon dioxide | vessels | nitrogen | oxygen | nutrients |
|---|---|---|---|---|
| particles | veins | arteries | capillaries | tubes |

Blood is vital to the working of the body.  It is carried around the body in blood

…………............…… . The blood is carried away from the heart in ………..............…… and

brought back in ………..............…… .  It supplies the tissues with ………..............…… and

………...........……… for energy, and carries ………..............…… to the lungs, where it is removed.

**Q2**  The **heart** keeps blood pumping around the body.

**a)**  The heart is a **double pump**.  Explain what this means.

......................................................................................................................................

**b)  i)**  What type of cell makes up the walls of the heart?

......................................................................................................................................

**ii)** Why is a blood supply to the cells in the walls of the heart essential?

......................................................................................................................................

**Q3**  The pictures below show cross sections of three **blood vessels** — an artery, a capillary and a vein.

A          B          C

**a)**  Write the name of each blood vessel by the correct letter.

A = .................................    B = .................................    C = .................................

**b)**  Explain how the following structures are related to the **function** of the blood vessel.

**i)**  Strong and elastic walls of arteries ....................................................................................

......................................................................................................................................

**ii)** Walls one cell thick in capillaries ....................................................................................

......................................................................................................................................

**iii)** Valves in veins ....................................................................................................................

......................................................................................................................................

# Heart Rate and Blood Pressure

**Q1** Fill in the blanks in the paragraph, choosing the correct words from the list below.

| lower | higher | stops | seventy | relaxes | artery | two | vein |
|---|---|---|---|---|---|---|---|

Blood pressure measurements record the pressure of the blood on the walls of an

.......................................... . When a doctor measures your blood pressure,

.......................................... readings are taken. The ..........................................

pressure is the pressure when your heart contracts. The other reading is the

pressure when your heart .......................................... .

**Q2** You can measure your **heart rate** by recording your **pulse rate**.
Explain why pulse rate can be used to measure heart rate.

..............................................................................................................................................

..............................................................................................................................................

**Q3** The table below shows the blood pressure measurements of five adult men.
**Normal blood pressure** is in the range of **90/60** to **120/80**.

| | Blood Pressure |
|---|---|
| Chris | 110/80 |
| Dan | 85/50 |
| Steve | 120/80 |
| Ahmed | 120/80 |
| Nigel | 150/95 |

**a)** How many men have blood pressure in the normal range? ..........................................

**b)** Explain why normal measurements are usually given as a range of values.

..............................................................................................................................................

**c)** Which of the men has high blood pressure? ..........................................

**d)** High blood pressure can damage arteries and cause the build up of fatty deposits.
Explain how **fatty deposits** in blood vessels could cause a **heart attack**.

..............................................................................................................................................

..............................................................................................................................................

..............................................................................................................................................

# Heart Disease

**Q1** Each of the factors below **increase** the **risk** of heart disease. Tick the correct boxes to show whether the each of the factors are **lifestyle** factors or **non-lifestyle** factors.

Lifestyle   Non-lifestyle

a) Poor diet ☐ ☐
b) Excessive alcohol intake ☐ ☐
c) Family history of heart disease ☐ ☐
d) Smoking ☐ ☐
e) Stress ☐ ☐

**Q2** Circle the correct word to complete the following sentence.

**Infrequent** / **Regular** moderate exercise reduces the risk of heart disease.

**Q3** Heart disease is more common in **industrialised** countries than in **non-industrialised** countries. Tick the box next to the explanation(s) below that you think are valid, reasonable explanations for this.

*Industrialised countries are the wealthy, developed countries, e.g. Britain and the US.*

☐ People in non-industrialised countries eat less junk food and so have a lower fat diet.

☐ Poorer people in non-industrialised countries will have to walk more because they cannot afford cars and so they get more exercise.

☐ Poorer people in non-industrialised countries cannot afford the treatment for heart disease and so are more likely to die of it.

**Q4 a)** What are **epidemiological studies**?

......................................................................................................................................

**b)** Suggest how epidemiological studies could be used to identify the lifestyle factors that increase the risk of heart disease.

......................................................................................................................................

......................................................................................................................................

......................................................................................................................................

*Module B2 — Keeping Healthy*

# Homeostasis — The Basics

**Q1**  Homeostasis is an important process in the human body.

a)  Define **homeostasis**.

.......................................................................................................................................

.......................................................................................................................................

b)  Why is homeostasis important for **cells** in the human body?

.......................................................................................................................................

c)  Hormonal communication systems are involved in homeostasis.
Name the **other** type of communication system involved.

.......................................................................................................................................

**Q2**  Write a definition of the term '**negative feedback**'.

.......................................................................................................................................

.......................................................................................................................................

**Q3**  The graph below shows how **negative feedback** systems operate in the body.

a)  Circle the correct word in each pair to complete the sentence below.

In a negative feedback system the response produced has the **opposite / same** effect

to the change detected — it **increases / reverses** the change.

b)  Fill in the missing words in the labels on the graph.

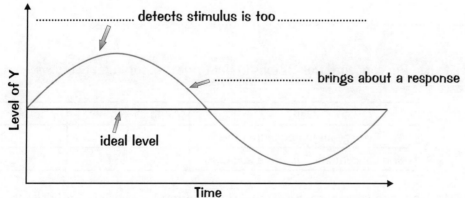

c)  What name is given to the part of a negative feedback system that receives information and
coordinates a response?

.......................................................................................................................................

# Controlling Water Content

**Q1** | The body needs to **balance** its water input and output.

**a)** Why is it important to maintain a balanced water level?

.................................................................................................................................................

**b)** Name three ways that water is **gained** by the body.

1. ..........................................................................................................................................

2. ..........................................................................................................................................

3. ..........................................................................................................................................

**Q2** | The concentration of a person's urine depends on the **concentration** of their **blood plasma**.

**a)** List three things that affect the concentration of **blood plasma**.

1. ..........................................................................................................................................

2. ..........................................................................................................................................

3. ..........................................................................................................................................

**b)** Complete the following sentences by circling the correct word(s).

**i)** When you drink too little you will produce **concentrated** / **dilute** urine.

**ii)** On a hot day you will produce **more concentrated** / **less concentrated** urine than on a cold day.

**iii)** Drinking a lot of water will produce a **large** / **small** amount of urine.

**c)** Why does **exercising** change the concentration of urine produced?

.................................................................................................................................................

.................................................................................................................................................

**Q3** | Mrs Finnegan had the **concentration of ions** in her **urine** measured on two days.

*Ion concentration is a measure of urine concentration.*

| Date | 6th December | 20th July |
|---|---|---|
| Average air temperature (°C) | 8 | 24 |
| Ion concentration in urine (mg/cm³) | 1.5 | 2.1 |

Assuming Mrs Finnegan consumes the same amount of food and drinks and does the same amount of exercise every day, suggest an explanation for the different ion concentrations in her urine.

.................................................................................................................................................

.................................................................................................................................................

# Controlling Water Content

**Q4**    The concentration of water in the blood is adjusted by the **kidneys**.
They ensure that the water content never gets **too high** or **too low**.

**a)**    What is the name given to the kind of mechanism by which water content is regulated?

...........................................................................................................................

**b)**    **ADH** is a chemical needed to control the body's water content.
What type of chemical is ADH?

The new kidney opera house was
less popular than the old one.

...........................................................................................

**c)**    Complete the diagram below by circling the correct word in each pair.

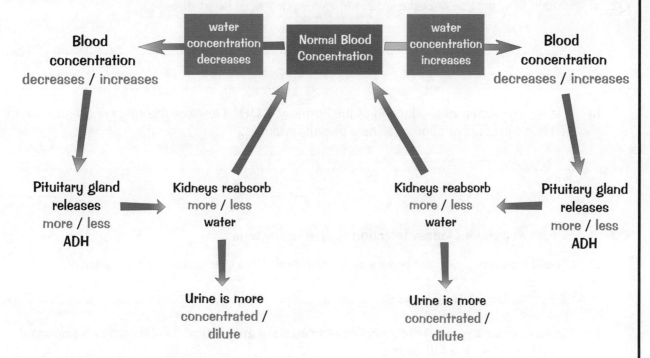

**Q5**    **Drugs** can affect the water content of the body.

**a)**    Circle the correct word from each pair to complete the passage about the effect of
**alcohol** on the water content of the body.

Alcohol **increases / decreases** the amount of ADH produced, causing the kidneys to

reabsorb **more / less** water than they usually do. This **increases / decreases** the amount of

water that leaves the body as **urine / sweat**, which can lead to **dehydration / overhydration**.

**b)**    Explain how the drug **ecstasy** can affect the quantity and concentration of urine produced.

...........................................................................................................................

...........................................................................................................................

---

**_Top Tips:_**    All this controlling water content stuff is pretty important. It's another example of
homeostasis and involves a nifty little negative feedback mechanism.

# Mixed Questions — Module B2

**Q1** Draw lines to match each of the **structures** below with its correct **function**.

| valves in veins | withstand the high pressure of blood leaving the heart |

| permeable walls of capillaries | allow the blood to exchange substances with cells |

| thick, elastic walls of arteries | keep blood flowing in the right direction |

HMS DRACULA

**Q2 a)** Explain how the use of **ecstasy** can increase your risk of **heart disease**.

.......................................................................................................................................

.......................................................................................................................................

**b)** Ecstasy also increases production of the hormone **ADH**. Describe the effect of an increase in ADH on the concentration of **urine** a person produces.

.......................................................................................................................................

**Q3** Helen has a **serious kidney infection** caused by **bacteria**.

**a)** Should Helen be given antibiotics as a treatment? Give one reason for your answer.

.......................................................................................................................................

**b)** Helen's doctor has given her a one-month course of **antibiotics**. Explain why it's important for Helen to take the **full course**.

.......................................................................................................................................

**c)** The bacteria responsible for Helen's infection produces a toxin that **blocks** the effect of **ADH** on the kidneys. What effect would this have on Helen's **urine** production?

.......................................................................................................................................

**d)** The bacteria that cause Helen's kidney infection can be grown in a laboratory. At 30 °C it takes **20 minutes** for **one** of the bacteria to reproduce. If **two** of the bacteria were left at this temperature in the laboratory for **100 minutes**, how many bacteria would there be?

.......................................................................................................................................

.......................................................................................................................................

.......................................................................................................................................

# Adaptation and Variation

**Q1** Give the definition of a **species**.

......................................................................................................

**Q2** There is **variation** between individuals of the same species. What kind of variation can be passed on to **offspring**?

......................................................................................................

big fish    little fish    cardboard box fish

**Q3 a)** Describe how **adaptations** to individuals help their species to survive in an environment.

......................................................................................................

......................................................................................................

**b)** Give three **adaptations** of an organism to its normal environment and describe how each of them helps it to survive.

1. ................................................................................................

......................................................................................................

2. ................................................................................................

......................................................................................................

3. ................................................................................................

......................................................................................................

**Q4** **Mutations** happen all the time and cause genetic variation.

**a)** What are mutations?

......................................................................................................

**b)** Give **one** possible effect of a mutation in the sex cells of an organism.

......................................................................................................

**Q5** Helen has skin cancer caused by a mutation that **damaged the DNA** in her skin cells. Since she developed cancer, Helen has had three children. None of her children have skin cancer. Explain why the mutation was **not** passed from Helen to her children.

......................................................................................................

......................................................................................................

# Natural Selection

**Q1** Tick the boxes to show whether the following statements are **true** or **false**.

| | True | False |
|---|---|---|
| **a)** Species become better and better suited to an environment due to natural selection. | ☐ | ☐ |
| **b)** Individuals compete for the resources they need to survive. | ☐ | ☐ |
| **c)** Organisms with a better chance of survival are less likely to pass on their genes. | ☐ | ☐ |

**Q2** The statements below explain the **process** of natural selection. Number the statements to put them in the correct order. The first and last stages have been done for you.

☐ This means more of the next generation have the characteristics which help them survive.

☐ These organisms have a better chance of survival.

☐ 1 Living things vary slightly from each other.

☐ 7 The species becomes better and better able to survive in its environment.

☐ Over several generations, the most advantageous features are naturally selected.

☐ Some variations make an organism better suited to its environment.

☐ The organisms which are more likely to survive are more likely to breed and pass on their genes.

**Q3** A farmer wants to produce larger tomatoes because it will help him to make more money. He selects the tomato plants that produce the largest tomatoes and breeds them together.

**a)** What is the process the farmer is using called?

.................................................................................................................................

**b)** How is this process different from natural selection?

.................................................................................................................................

.................................................................................................................................

.................................................................................................................................

**Top Tips:** Selective breeding's a dead useful bit of science that we've been using for yonks — farmers use it to get the most useful varieties of plants and animals. All you need to know for the exam is how it's different from natural selection — but that means you need to know all about natural selection too. Oh well, at least learning all of this stuff should keep you out of trouble for a while...

# Natural Selection

**Q4**   **Sickle cell anaemia** is a serious **genetic** disease that makes it harder for a person to carry enough oxygen in their blood.  In Europe the disease is very **rare**.  However, in Africa sickle cell anaemia is more **common**.

a)   Explain why natural selection may act **against** people with sickle cell anaemia in Europe.

........................................................................................................................................................................

........................................................................................................................................................................

b)   **Malaria** is a disease that kills huge numbers of people in Africa.  People who are **carriers** of sickle cell anaemia are **more resistant** to malaria.  Explain how natural selection means there is more sickle cell anaemia in Africa.

*Carriers of sickle cell anaemia have one copy of the allele for the disorder, but they don't show the symptoms.*

........................................................................................................................................................................

........................................................................................................................................................................

**Q5**   There are two varieties of **peppered moth** — one with light wings with dark spots, and one with dark wings and light spots.  The graph below shows the population of each type of moth found in woodland near Manchester.

**Light Moth  Dark Moth**

a)   Briefly describe how the population of the two types changed over the time shown on the graph.

i)   **Light** moth: ...........................................................................

......................................................................................................

ii)  **Dark** moth: ...........................................................................

......................................................................................................

b)   It is thought that the changes in the population sizes resulted from pollution from the Industrial Revolution darkening the bark of trees.

i)   Which type of moth would be better hidden from predators by darker trees? ...........................

ii)  Explain how this might have led to the change in population sizes seen on the graph.

........................................................................................................................................................................

........................................................................................................................................................................

........................................................................................................................................................................

c)   If the Industrial Revolution hadn't occurred, would the population sizes of the two moth species still have changed?  Explain your answer.

........................................................................................................................................................................

........................................................................................................................................................................

# *Evolution*

**Q1** Life on **Earth** is incredibly **varied**.

**a)** How long ago is life on Earth thought to have begun?  Circle the correct answer.

**350 thousand years     3500 million years     3500 billion years**

**b)** Circle the correct word in each pair to complete the following sentence.

All species on Earth today **grew / evolved** from very **simple / complex** living things.

**Q2)** Tick the boxes to show whether the following statements are **true** or **false**.

| | True | False |
|---|---|---|
| **a)** Scientists have found evidence for evolution by looking at fossils. | ☐ | ☐ |
| **b)** Fossils show that species have become simpler as time has gone on. | ☐ | ☐ |
| **c)** Similarities and differences in DNA show evolutionary relationships. | ☐ | ☐ |
| **d)** The more distantly related two species are, the more different their DNA is. | ☐ | ☐ |

**Q3 a)** Complete the following sentence by circling the correct word in each pair.

Darwin came up with the theory of evolution by **natural selection / sustainability** by making **many / few** observations of organisms and applying **creative thought / foolishness** to his findings.

**b)** A man called **Lamarck** also had a theory about how evolution happened.

**i)** Briefly describe Lamarck's theory.

.................................................................................................................................

.................................................................................................................................

**ii)** Give **one** reason why Lamarck's theory was rejected in favour of Darwin's theory.

.................................................................................................................................

**Q4** Completely **new species** occasionally develop when certain factors combine.

**a)** Which **three** of these factors can help to produce a new species?  Circle the correct answers.

velocity

environmental change              mutations         natural selection

predictions                        extinctions

**b)** Explain how each of the factors you chose can contribute to the development of a new species.

1. ..........................................................................................................................

2. ..........................................................................................................................

3. ..........................................................................................................................

**c)** Give one other factor that can lead to the formation of a new species.

.................................................................................................................................

# Biodiversity and Classification

**Q1**  Tick the boxes to indicate whether the following statements are **true** or **false**.

|  | True | False |
|---|---|---|
| **a)** A species is said to be extinct when there are no more individuals of that species. | ☐ | ☐ |
| **b)** Some extinctions have been caused by human activity. | ☐ | ☐ |
| **c)** The rate at which species are becoming extinct is slowing down. | ☐ | ☐ |

**Q2**  Maintaining the Earth's **biodiversity** is very important.

**a)** 'Biodiversity' means the variety of life on Earth.
Suggest three types of variety that it includes.

1. .................................................................................................................................

2. .................................................................................................................................

3. .................................................................................................................................

**b)** Give two reasons why maintaining biodiversity is important.

1. .................................................................................................................................

.................................................................................................................................

2. .................................................................................................................................

.................................................................................................................................

**Q3**  All organisms can be **classified** into groups, based on their similarities and differences.

**a)** As you go from kingdom to species, what happens to:

**i)** the number of **types** of organism in each group?

.................................................................................................................................

**ii)** the number of **characteristics** the organisms in each group have in common?

.................................................................................................................................

**b)** Give two types of characteristic that can be used to group organisms together.

1. .................................................................................................................................

2. .................................................................................................................................

# Interactions Between Organisms

**Q1**    The resources below are **essential** for life.

a)  Draw lines to connect the boxes to show which resources are essential for plants, essential for animals and essential for both.

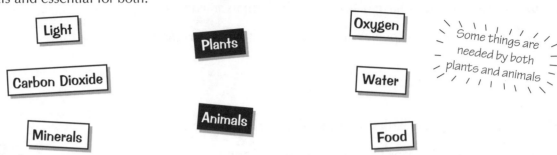

b)  What would happen if an essential resource was in short supply?

...........................................................................................................................................

c)  Give one way that organisms are dependent on other species for their survival.

...........................................................................................................................................

**Q2**    The **deercat** is a species that lives only in the forest of Hamilton. The following table shows the number of **deercat** in the forest over a period of **five years**.

| Year | 2006 | 2007 | 2008 | 2009 | 2010 |
|---|---|---|---|---|---|
| Number of deercat | 55 | 38 | 19 | 8 | 0 |

a)  Calculate the mean number of deercat over the 5 year period.

...........................................................................................................................................

...........................................................................................................................................

b)  In 2010 the deercat became extinct.

i)  What does 'extinct' mean?

.......................................................................................................................................

ii) Rapid environmental change can cause a species to become extinct.
Suggest three changes which could have caused the extinction of the deercat.

1. ..............................................................................................................................

2. ..............................................................................................................................

3. ..............................................................................................................................

# Interactions Between Organisms

**Q3** The diagram below shows a **woodland food web**. Last year a chemical was spilt in the woods which was poisonous to voles. The population of **voles** significantly **decreased**.

a) Suggest an explanation for each of the following consequences:

i) The population of barn owls **decreasing**.

......................................................................

ii) The population of insects **increasing**.

......................................................................

iii) The population of insects **decreasing**.

......................................................................

b) Suggest what might happen to the **thrush population**. Give a reason for your answer.

......................................................................

......................................................................

**Q4** The diagram shows part of a food web from Nebraska in the USA. The **flowerhead weevil** doesn't occur naturally in this area. It was introduced by **farmers** to eat the musk thistle which is a weed.

a) Why might the introduction of the flowerhead weevil decrease the number of platte thistles?

......................................................................

b) What effect will a decrease in the number of platte thistles have on the amount of wild honey produced in the area? Give a reason for your answer.

......................................................................

......................................................................

......................................................................

c) Suggest a reason why the population of platte thistles may increase as the population of musk thistles is reduced by the introduction of flowerhead weevils.

......................................................................

......................................................................

**Top Tips:** Interdependence is just like happy families — dad relies on mum, the kids rely on mum and dad, mum relies on Auntie Nora... Families don't tend to eat each other though, so it's not quite the same — my sister looks like she wants to eat me sometimes, but I don't think she will.

# Energy in an Ecosystem

**Q1**    Complete the sentences below by circling the correct words.

*leaf it out*

a)    Nearly all life on Earth depends on **food** / **energy** from the Sun.

b)    Plants absorb a **small** / **large** percentage of the Sun's energy for **photosynthesis** / **respiration**.

c)    To obtain energy animals must **decay** / **eat** plant material or other animals.

d)    Decay organisms **obtain** / **lose** energy when they feed on parts of **living** / **dead** organisms.

e)    Parts of a dead organism that remain **uneaten** / **unwashed** cause energy to be lost from a food chain.

**Q2**    A **food chain** is shown in the diagram.

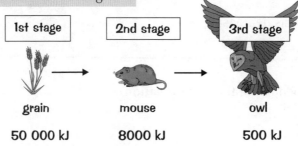

| 1st stage | 2nd stage | 3rd stage |
|---|---|---|
| grain | mouse | owl |
| 50 000 kJ | 8000 kJ | 500 kJ |

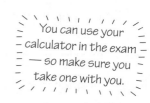
*You can use your calculator in the exam — so make sure you take one with you.*

a)    Calculate the **amount** of energy lost between the:

   i)   1st and 2nd stages. ........................................................................

   ii)  2nd and 3rd stages. .......................................................................

b)    Calculate the **efficiency** of energy transfer from the:

   i)   1st to 2nd stages. .........................................................................

   ii)  2nd to 3rd stages. ........................................................................

**Q3**    Study the diagram of **energy transfer** shown.

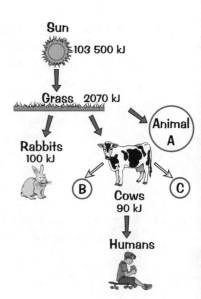

a)    Using the figures on the diagram, calculate the **efficiency** of energy transfer from the **Sun** to the **grass**.

   ..................................................................................

b)    The **efficiency** of energy transfer from the grass to the next stage is **10%**. Work out how much energy is available in **animal A**.

   ..................................................................................

c)    **B** and **C** are processes that represent energy loss. Suggest what these processes might be.

   ..................................................................................

d)    Why do food chains rarely have more than five stages?

   ..................................................................................

   ..................................................................................

*Module B3 — Life on Earth*

# The Carbon Cycle

**Q1**    **Carbon** is a very important element that is constantly being recycled.

a) What is the one way that carbon is removed from the atmosphere?

.................................................................................................................

b) In what form is carbon removed from the atmosphere?

.................................................................................................................

c) What is the role of microorganisms in the carbon cycle?

.................................................................................................................

d) How is carbon from plants passed on through the food chain?

.................................................................................................................

e) By what process do **all** living organisms return carbon to the air?

.................................................................................................................

**Q2**    The diagram below shows a version of the **carbon cycle**.

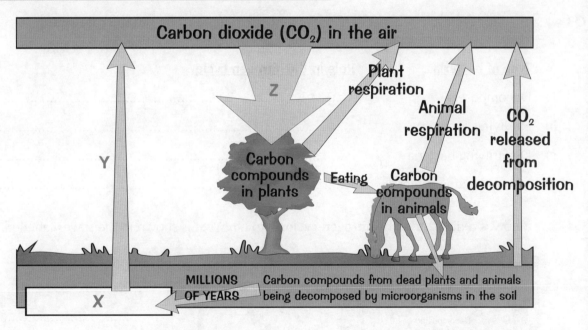

a) Name substance **X** shown on the diagram above.  .................................................

b) Name the process labelled **Y** on the diagram above.  .............................................

c) Name the process labelled **Z** on the diagram above.  .............................................

___

**_Top Tips:_**    Don't get stressed out if there's a carbon cycle question in your exam paper and the cycle doesn't look like the one above — there are a few different ways to draw it. But if you know what's going on in one version of a carbon cycle, you know what's going on in all of them. Phew.

# The Nitrogen Cycle

**Q1**   Match up each type of **organism** below with the way it obtains **nitrogen**.

| Plants | By eating other organisms |

| Animals | By absorbing nitrates from the soil |

**Q2**   **Nitrogen** gas has to be fixed into nitrates before plants can use it.

**a)**   What do plants use nitrogen for?

..............................................................................................................................

**b)**   Give two ways that nitrogen gas is fixed into nitrates.

1. ...........................................................................................................................

2. ...........................................................................................................................

**c)**   Ammonia can also be turned into nitrates by bacteria.  What is this process called?

..............................................................................................................................

**Q3**   The nitrogen cycle is dependent on a number of different types of **microorganism**.
Explain the role of each of the following types of **bacteria** in the nitrogen cycle.

| **Type of bacteria** | **Role in the nitrogen cycle** |
|---|---|
| **a)** Decomposers | ..................................................................................... |
| **b)** Nitrifying bacteria | ..................................................................................... |
| **c)** Denitrifying bacteria | ..................................................................................... |
| **d)** Nitrogen-fixing bacteria | ..................................................................................... |

**Q4**   Below is a diagram of the **nitrogen cycle**.  Explain what is shown in the stages labelled:

**a)**   X .......................................................
...........................................................
...........................................................

**b)**   Y .......................................................
...........................................................
...........................................................

**c)**   Z .......................................................
...........................................................
...........................................................

# Measuring Environmental Change

**Q1** Tick the boxes to indicate whether the following statements are **true** or **false**.

| | | True | False |
|---|---|---|---|
| **a)** | Changes in the environment can be measured with non-living indicators. | ☐ | ☐ |
| **b)** | A low level of nitrates in a river could suggest pollution by fertilisers. | ☐ | ☐ |
| **c)** | Changes in $CO_2$ level don't indicate an environmental change. | ☐ | ☐ |
| **d)** | Changes in climate can be shown by long-term temperature measurements. | ☐ | ☐ |

**Q2** **Mayfly nymphs** and **sludge worms** are often used to measure environmental change.

**a)** What is the name for an organism used in this way? ....................................................................

Juanita recorded the number of each species in water samples taken at three different distances away from a sewage outlet. Her results are shown on the right.

| Distance (km) | No. of mayfly nymphs | No. of sludge worms |
|---|---|---|
| 1 | 3 | 20 |
| 2 | 11 | 14 |
| 3 | 23 | 7 |

**b)** What can you conclude about the two organisms from these results?

......................................................................................................................................................

......................................................................................................................................................

**c)** Bacteria found in water can use up lots of oxygen. Sewage causes bacterial populations in water to increase. Suggest why sewage may **decrease** the number of mayfly nymphs.

......................................................................................................................................................

......................................................................................................................................................

**Q3)** Maria recorded the average **percentage** cover of **lichen** on sections of tree trunks in five different locations. Each location was a different **distance** from the **industrial city** of Beanton.

**a)** Which location has the highest average percentage cover of lichen?

..................................

| Location | A | B | C | D | E |
|---|---|---|---|---|---|
| Distance from Beanton (km) | 5 | 10 | 15 | 20 | 25 |
| Average percentage cover of lichen (%) | 21 | 30 | 35 | 42 | 49 |

**b)** **i)** Describe the trend shown in Maria's data.

......................................................................................................................................................

**ii)** Suggest a reason for this trend.

......................................................................................................................................................

......................................................................................................................................................

# Sustainability

**Q1**   Give a definition of **sustainability**.

.................................................................................................................................................

.................................................................................................................................................

**Q2**   Complete the following passage by choosing the correct words from those given.

| biodegradable | landfill | less energy | more packaging | transporting |
| thrown away | less pollution | damages | yodelling | recycled |

One of the ways of making packaging materials more sustainable is to use

..................................... materials that rot away more quickly than things

like plastics.  This causes ..................................... .  Another way is to use

..................................... packaging materials, which uses

..................................... than producing new materials.  This is more

sustainable because energy production ..................................... the

environment.  However, the most sustainable thing to do is to use fewer

packaging materials.  This is because making and .....................................

the materials always requires energy.

**Q3**   A farmer produces potatoes for a large supermarket chain.
He **only grows potatoes** in his fields.

**a)**   What name is given to this method of crop production?

.................................................................................................................................................

**b)**   Is this method of crop production **sustainable**?  Explain your answer.

...........................................................................................................

...........................................................................................................

*You'll need to talk about biodiversity in your answer.*

...........................................................................................................

...........................................................................................................

---

**Top Tips:**   Sustainability is the reason why supermarkets are stingy with their carrier bags.
Carrier bags are made from plastic which takes ages to decompose — by using fewer carrier bags we're
helping to preserve the world's resources and cause less pollution.

# Mixed Questions — Module B3

**Q1**    As human populations have increased, the number of species **extinctions** has also increased.

What does this correlation suggest?

.................................................................................................................................................

.................................................................................................................................................

**Q2**    A farmer grows a crop that has been created by **selective breeding**. The crop is grown with a **nitrate-rich fertiliser**, but it's thought that the fertiliser has **polluted** a local river.

**a)**    What is **selective breeding**?

.................................................................................................................................................

**b)**    Describe how you could check to see if the river has been polluted by the fertiliser.

.................................................................................................................................................

.................................................................................................................................................

**Q3**    An **aquatic food chain** is shown.

plankton → shrimp → small fish → carp

100 000 kJ        ..........................        1000 kJ        ..........................

**a)**    Suggest two possible ways that the small fish is **adapted** to its aquatic environment.

1. ......................................................................................................................................

2. ......................................................................................................................................

**b)**    90 000 kJ is lost between the 1st stage (plankton) and the 2nd stage (shrimp).

**i)**    On the diagram, write the amount of energy available in the shrimp for the small fish.

**ii)**    Calculate the **efficiency** of energy transfer from the 1st to the 2nd stage of the food chain.

.................................................................................................................................................

**c)**    The energy transfer from the small fish to the carp is **5%** efficient.

**i)**    On the diagram, write the amount of **energy** available in the **carp**.

**ii)**    How much energy is **lost** from the food chain at this stage?

.................................................................................................................................................

# Cell Structure and Function

**Q1**    Draw lines to match the **enzymes** for different reactions to where they're found in a **plant cell**.

| Enzymes for aerobic respiration are found in... | | the cytoplasm |
|---|---|---|
| Enzymes for anaerobic respiration are found in... | | mitochondria |
| Enzymes for photosynthesis are found in... | | chloroplasts |

**Q2**    Complete each statement below by circling the correct word(s) from each pair.

a)    The reactions of **anaerobic** / **aerobic** respiration occur in the **mitochondria** / **chloroplasts**.

b)    The **cell membrane** / **nucleus** allows water and gases to pass freely in and out of a cell.

c)    **Proteins** / **DNA molecules** are made in the **chloroplasts** / **cytoplasm**.

**Q3**    Fill in the blanks in the passage using the words provided below.
Some words can be used more than once.

| proteins | nucleus | chlorophyll | enzymes |
|---|---|---|---|

DNA is found in the ................................. . It contains the instructions for making

................................., for example the ................................. involved in photosynthesis,

which are found in chloroplasts along with ................................. .

**Q4**    Place a tick in the table to show the different parts that are
found in each cell type.  Some have been done for you.

| | Animal cell | Yeast cell | Bacterial cell |
|---|---|---|---|
| **Nucleus** | ✔ | | |
| **Cytoplasm** | | | ✔ |
| **Cell membrane** | | | |
| **Cell wall** | | ✔ | |
| **Mitochondria** | | | |
| **Circular DNA molecule** | | | |

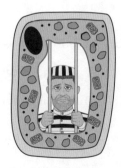

---

**Top Tips:**    If there's one thing you need to know inside out and back to front it's cells,
because all the other stuff that crops up in Module B4 involves them in some way.  When it comes
to life's fundamental processes, cells are pretty much the hippest place to be.  Really.

# Enzymes

**Q1 a)** Write a definition of the word '**enzyme**'.

..............................................................................................................................................................

**b)** Complete the following sentence:

Enzymes are made from ................................. that are carried in genes.

**c)** What is the name of the area of an enzyme where the substrate joins and the reaction occurs?

..............................................................................................................................................................

**d)** In the box below, draw a series of labelled sketches to show the **lock and key model**.

**Q2** This graph shows the results from an investigation into the effect of **temperature** on the rate of an **enzyme-controlled** reaction.

**a)** What is the **optimum** temperature for this enzyme?

..........................................................................................

**b)** Tick the box next to the statement which correctly describes the results shown in the graph.

The rate of reaction increased until the enzyme was used up. ☐

The rate of reaction increased with increasing temperature up to the enzyme's optimum temperature. ☐

**c)** Explain what happens to the enzyme at **45 °C**.

..............................................................................................................................................

..............................................................................................................................................

..............................................................................................................................................

I'm melting, melting. What a world, what a cruel, cruel world.

enzyme

*Module B4 — The Processes of Life*

# <u>Enzymes</u>

**Q3** Stuart has a sample of an enzyme and he is trying to find out what its **optimum pH** is. Stuart tests the enzyme by **timing** how long it takes to break down a substance at different pHs. The results of Stuart's experiment are shown below.

| pH | time taken for reaction in seconds |
|----|------------------------------------|
| 2  | 101 |
| 4  | 83  |
| 6  | 17  |
| 8  | 76  |
| 10 | 99  |
| 12 | 102 |

**a)** Draw a line graph of the results on the grid below.

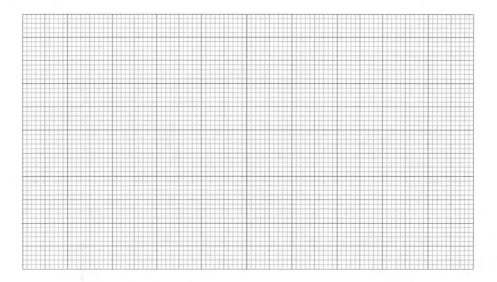

**b)** Roughly what is the **optimum pH** for the enzyme?

......................................................................................................................................

**c)** Explain why the reaction is very slow at certain pHs.

......................................................................................................................................

......................................................................................................................................

**d)** Would you expect to find this enzyme in the **stomach**? Explain your answer.

.................................................................................................................

*The stomach has a low pH.*

......................................................................................................................................

**_Top Tips:_** Enzymes crop up all the time in Biology so it's worth spending plenty of time making sure you know all the basics. This stuff is also dead useful if you end up sitting next to someone with Desirability for a middle name at a dinner party — nobody can resist a bit of optimum pH chat.

# Aerobic Respiration

**Q1** Tick the correct boxes to show whether the sentences are **true** or **false**.

|  | True | False |
|---|---|---|
| a) Respiration is a series of chemical reactions that release energy. | ☐ | ☐ |
| b) Large food molecules are made by respiration. | ☐ | ☐ |
| c) Aerobic respiration releases more energy than anaerobic respiration. | ☐ | ☐ |
| d) Aerobic respiration requires oxygen. | ☐ | ☐ |
| e) Breathing is a kind of respiration. | ☐ | ☐ |
| f) Microorganisms do not respire aerobically. | ☐ | ☐ |

**Q2** Use the words and symbols given to complete the word and symbol equations for **aerobic respiration**.

oxygen    6CO₂    6H₂O

water    6O₂    glucose

I told you aerobic respiration made energy.

Do you think anyone will notice I blew up the house?

word: ........................ + ........................ → carbon dioxide + ........................ (+ energy)

symbol: $C_6H_{12}O_6$ + ........................ → ........................ + ........................ (+ energy)

**Q3** The **energy** released by **respiration** is used to make **large molecules** (polymers) from smaller ones.

a) Describe how two different polymers are synthesised using the energy released by respiration.

1. ........................................................................................................

........................................................................................................

2. ........................................................................................................

........................................................................................................

b) Give two other processes that use the energy released by respiration.

1. ........................................................................................................

2. ........................................................................................................

# *Anaerobic Respiration*

**Q1**    Complete the following sentences by circling the correct word(s).

a)    Anaerobic respiration takes place in animal and plant cells and
some microorganisms when there is **lots of** / **little or no** oxygen.

b)    Plant roots respire anaerobically in **dry** / **waterlogged** soil.

c)    Only bacteria that respire anaerobically can survive **under** / **on top** of your skin.

d)    During **vigorous** / **gentle** exercise your muscle cells respire anaerobically
because the body can't get enough oxygen to them fast enough.

**Q2**    Anaerobic respiration produces different **products** in different cells.

a)    Use the words given below to complete the **word equations** for anaerobic respiration below.
You may need to use some of the words more than once.

| carbon dioxide | ethanol | energy | glucose |

i)  Plant cells:    glucose → .............................. + .............................. (+ ..............................)

ii) Animal cells:  .............................. → **lactic acid** (+ ..............................)

b)    Name the two **chemicals** that are produced by anaerobic respiration in **yeast**:

1. ...................................................................................................................................

2. ...................................................................................................................................

**Q3**    **Fermentation** is when microorganisms break down sugars
into other products by respiring anaerobically.  Describe how
fermentation is used to produce the following:

a)    Biogas

.......................................................................................................

.......................................................................................................

.......................................................................................................

b)    Bread

.......................................................................................................

.......................................................................................................

c)    Alcohol

.......................................................................................................

---

*Module B4 — The Processes of Life*

# Photosynthesis

**Q1**  **Photosynthesis** takes place in plant cells and in some microorganisms.

a) What is photosynthesis?

.................................................................................................................................

b) Use some of the words below to complete the word equation for photosynthesis.

carbon dioxide          nitrogen          water          glucose          sodium chloride

light energy

......................... + ......................... $\xrightarrow{}$ ......................... + oxygen

c) Use some of the symbols below to complete the symbol equation for photosynthesis.

$6O_2$          $6N_2$          $6H_2O$          $C_6H_{12}O_6$          $6NaCl$

light energy

$6CO_2$ + ......................... $\xrightarrow{}$ ......................... + .........................

d) Draw lines to match each word below to its correct description.

chlorophyll          a green substance needed for photosynthesis

oxygen          the food that is produced by photosynthesis

sunlight          a waste product of photosynthesis

glucose          supplies the energy for photosynthesis

**Q2**  Plants use the **glucose** produced by photosynthesis for many things. Complete the following passage using some of the words provided.

cellulose          nitrogen          soil          energy          chlorophyll          starch

Plants use glucose in respiration to release ............................... . Plants convert

glucose into ............................... for storage.  Glucose is also converted into

substances like ............................... and ............................... . It can also be

combined with ............................... from nitrates taken up from the

............................... and used to make amino acids.

**Q3**  Explain why organisms that photosynthesise form the start of **food chains**.

.................................................................................................................................

.................................................................................................................................

# Rate of Photosynthesis

**Q1**  State what a **limiting factor** of photosynthesis is.

.................................................................................................................................

**Q2**  Seth investigated the effect of different concentrations of **carbon dioxide** on the rate of photosynthesis of his Swiss cheese plant. He measured the rate of photosynthesis with increasing light intensity at **three** different $CO_2$ concentrations. The results are shown on the graph below.

**a)** What effect does increasing the concentration of $CO_2$ have on the rate of photosynthesis? Use the graph and your own knowledge.

..........................................................................

..........................................................................

..........................................................................

**b)** Explain why all the lines level off eventually.

...................................................................................................

...................................................................................................

*Think about a third limiting factor.*

**Q3**  Lucy investigated the **volume of oxygen** produced by pondweed at **different intensities of light**. Her results are shown in the table below.

| Relative light intensity | 1 | 2 | 3 | 4 | 5 |
|---|---|---|---|---|---|
| Volume of oxygen produced in 10 minutes (ml) | 12 | 25 | 37 | 48 | 61 |

**a)** Plot a graph of her results.

**b)** Describe the relationship shown on the graph between light intensity and photosynthesis rate.

.................................................................

.................................................................

.................................................................

**c)** Would you expect this relationship to continue if Lucy continued to increase the light intensity? Explain your answer.

.................................................................

.................................................................

# <u>*Rate of Photosynthesis*</u>

**Q4** The rate of photosynthesis in some pondweed was recorded by counting the number of bubbles of oxygen produced per minute at equal intervals during the day.

| No. bubbles per minute | Time of day |
|---|---|
| 10 | 06.00 |
| 20 | 12.00 |
| 10 | 18.00 |
| 0 | |

**a)** The time for the final reading is missing.
Predict what the time is likely to be.

..................................................................................

**b)** Explain why the rate of photosynthesis is 0 bubbles per minute for this time of day.

..........................................................................

..........................................................................

**c)** Plot a **bar graph** on the grid on the right to display the results shown in the table.

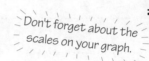
*Don't forget about the scales on your graph.*

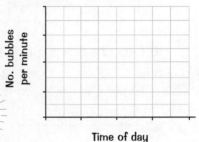

No. bubbles per minute

Time of day

**Q5** The table shows the average daytime summer **temperatures** in different habitats around the world.

| Habitat | Temperature (°C) |
|---|---|
| Forest | 19 |
| Arctic | 0 |
| Desert | 32 |
| Grassland | 22 |
| Rainforest | 27 |

**a)** Plot a **bar chart** for these results on the grid.

**b)** From the temperatures, in which area would you expect the smallest number of plants to grow?

..................................................................................................................................

**c)** Suggest a reason for your answer above using the terms **enzymes** and **photosynthesis**.

..................................................................................................................................

..................................................................................................................................

**Q6** Farmer Fred doesn't put his cows out during the winter because the grass is **not growing**.

**a)** Give **one** difference between summer and winter conditions that affects the rate of photosynthesis.

..................................................................................................................................

**b)** How are the rate of photosynthesis and the growth rate of the grass related?

..................................................................................................................................

..................................................................................................................................

48

# Investigating Photosynthesis

**Q1** Sandy is investigating the effect of **light** on the distribution of a plant species. She's thinking about the things she could use to help her collect data.

**a)** Name a piece of equipment Sandy could use to measure the level of light.

..............................................................................................................

**b)** Sandy decides to use a **quadrat** in her investigation.

**i)** What is a quadrat?

..............................................................................................................

**ii)** Describe how a quadrat can be used to estimate the **percentage cover** of a plant species.

..............................................................................................................

..............................................................................................................

**c)** In her investigation Sandy uses a **transect**.

**i)** What are transects used for?

..............................................................................................................

**ii)** Put the following stages in the correct order to describe how to take a transect by writing numbers in the boxes next to them.

☐ Start at one end of the tape measure and collect your data.

☐ Keep moving along the tape measure and collecting your data until the other end is reached.

☐ Run a tape measure between two fixed points.

☐ Move along the tape measure and collect your data again.

**d)** Sandy carries out her investigation and she finds a type of plant that she doesn't recognise. Use the key to **identify** the plant from the sample shown below.

| 1. Does the plant have seeds? | Yes – go to 2. |
| | No – go to 3. |
| 2. Does the plant have flowers? | Yes – it is a flowering plant. |
| | No – it is a conifer. |
| 3. Does the plant have long stems with lots of small leaves? | Yes – it is a fern. |
| | No – it is a moss. |

Type of plant: ...................................................

*Module B4 — The Processes of Life*

# Diffusion, Osmosis and Active Transport

**Q1** Complete the passage below by circling the correct word in each pair.

> Diffusion is the **active / passive** overall movement of molecules from a region of
> their **higher / lower** concentration to a region of their **higher / lower** concentration.
> For example, the movement of **carbon dioxide and oxygen / water and salts**
> in and out of plant leaves happens by diffusion.

**Q2** Look at the diagram and answer the questions below.

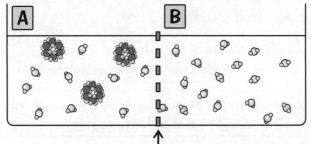

Partially permeable membrane

**a)** On which side of the membrane is there the **highest** concentration of water molecules?

..........................................................................................................................................

**b)** Predict whether the level of liquid on side **B** will **rise** or **fall** over time. Explain your answer.

The liquid level on side B will ...................., because ..........................................

..........................................................................................................................................

**Q3** **Active transport** is an important process that takes place in living organisms.

**a)** Define active transport.

..........................................................................................................................................

..........................................................................................................................................

**b)** Give an example of active transport in plants.

..........................................................................................................................................

**Top Tips:** Osmosis, active transport and diffusion are some of the ways that things can move in and out of your cells. Osmosis and diffusion just simply happen without any help, whereas active transport needs a helping hand — it needs energy to get stuff moving.

# Mixed Questions — Module B4

**Q1**  Circle the correct word equation for **aerobic respiration**.

glucose + oxygen → carbon dioxide + water (+ energy)

protein + oxygen → carbon dioxide + water (+ energy)

glucose + carbon dioxide → oxygen + water (+ energy)

**Q2**  **Diffusion** and **osmosis** are ways that molecules move into and out of cells.

**a)**  Connect the term with the correct definition by drawing a line.

Diffusion

the overall movement of water from a dilute to a more concentrated solution through a partially permeable membrane.

Osmosis

the passive overall movement of particles from a region of their higher concentration to region of their lower concentration

diffusion is an essential life process

**b)**  Give **one** example of osmosis in plants.

..........................................................................................................................

**Q3**  Plants use photosynthesis to produce **glucose**.

**a)  i)**  Name the other **product** of photosynthesis

..........................................................................................................................

**ii)**  Name the two **reactants** of photosynthesis.

1. ....................................................................................................................

2. ....................................................................................................................

**b)**  List three things that plants use glucose for.

1. ....................................................................................................................

2. ....................................................................................................................

3. ....................................................................................................................

**c)**  Give **one** example of another organism that uses photosynthesis to produce glucose.

..........................................................................................................................

# Mixed Questions — Module B4

**Q4** Graham is growing flowers in his greenhouse. Their **rate** of **photosynthesis**, and so rate of growth, **slows** during the **winter**.

a) Circle **two** factors below that limit the rate of photosynthesis.

length of a plant's roots      amount of soil

amount of light      amount of carbon dioxide

Photo-Synthesis Studios

Specialists in photos of:
• families on sheepskin rugs.
• people in poses they'd never normally strike.
• wannabe models.

Special offer Buy one frame, get one free.

b) Name **one** other factor that can limit the rate of photosynthesis.

..................................................................................................................

c) Graham wants to speed up the rate of growth of his flowers.
What could Graham add to his greenhouse in the **winter** for better growth?

..................................................................................................................

**Q5** **Enzymes** are involved in lots of chemical reactions.

a) Tick the correct boxes to show whether the sentences are **true** or **false**.

**True False**

i) Most enzymes are made of fat. ☐ ☐

ii) Enzymes need a specific constant temperature to work at their optimum. ☐ ☐

iii) The active site is where the substrate joins onto the enzyme. ☐ ☐

iv) A denatured enzyme is an enzyme that's been artificially manufactured. ☐ ☐

v) One enzyme can speed up a lot of different reactions. ☐ ☐

b) Write the correct version of each false sentence below.

..................................................................................................................

..................................................................................................................

..................................................................................................................

c) Where in a **plant cell** are the enzymes found that are involved in:

i) aerobic respiration?

..................................................................................................................

ii) photosynthesis?

..................................................................................................................

# DNA — Making Proteins

**Q1** The following questions are about **DNA**.

**a)** What name is given to the **shape** of a DNA molecule?

~~helix~~ double helix

**b)** How many different bases make up the DNA structure?

four

**c)** Which bases pair up together?

Adenine and thymine , Guanine & Cytosine

**Q2** Tick the boxes to show whether the following statements are **true** or **false**.

| | True | False |
|---|---|---|
| **a)** Genes are sections of DNA that code for specific proteins. | ✓ | |
| **b)** Each amino acid is coded for by a set of four base pairs. | ✓ | |
| **c)** DNA is found in the cytoplasm of plant and animal cells. | | ✓ |
| **d)** Proteins are made in the cytoplasm of plant and animal cells. | ✓ | |
| **e)** Messenger RNA carries information from the DNA into the cytoplasm. | ✓ | |
| **f)** Messenger RNA molecules have two strands. | | ✓ |

**Q3** The order of bases in a gene determines the **sequence** of **amino acids** in a protein.

**a)** **i)** On the section of DNA shown complete the lower sequence of bases.

A G G C T A G C C A A T C G C C G A A G C T C A
T C C G A T C G G T T A G C G G C T T C G A G T

**ii)** Calculate how many **amino acids** this section of DNA codes for.

8

**b)** Using the information in the table complete the amino acid sequence for the following messenger RNA sequence. The first two have been done for you.

~~CGAAAGGCCGAAGAAAGCCGCCG~~

2   3   1   4   4   3   1   1

| Triplet | Amino Acid Reference Number |
|---|---|
| GCG | 1 |
| CGA | 2 |
| AAG | 3 |
| GAA | 4 |

# Cell Division — Mitosis

**Q1** Complete the following passage using some of the words below.

~~genetically~~   four   egg   ~~copies~~
~~two~~   growth   damaged   ~~parent~~

Mitosis is where a cell divides into ...two... cells. These new cells are
...genetically.... identical to each other and the ...parent... cell.
Before a cell divides, it ...copies... its DNA. Organisms use mitosis
for ...growth... and to replace ...damaged... cells.

**Q2** Tick the boxes to show whether the following statements are **true** or **false**.

True  False

a) As a cell grows the number of organelles increases. ☑ ☐

b) Before mitosis the chromosomes are copied so that the cell has four copies of its DNA. ☐ ☑

c) When chromosomes are copied the strands of a DNA molecule separate so that new strands can form next to them. ☑ ☑

**Q3** The following diagram shows the different stages of **mitosis**. Write a short description to explain each stage. The first one has been done for you.

The cell's DNA duplicates and forms X-shaped chromosomes. Each arm of a chromosome is exactly the same as the other.

a) Line up and cell fibres pull them apart.

b) Membrane forms around each set of chromosomes these became nuclei.

c) 2 geneticly identicy cells.

# Cell Division — Meiosis

**Q1** Tick the boxes below to show which statements are true of **mitosis**, **meiosis** or **both**.

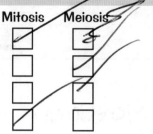

| | Mitosis | Meiosis |
|---|---|---|
| a) Halves the number of chromosomes. | ☑ | ☑ |
| b) Is a type of cell division. | ☐ | ☐ |
| c) Forms cells that are genetically different. | ☐ | ☐ |
| d) In humans, it only happens in the reproductive organs. | ☐ | ☐ |

**Q2** The diagram shows the formation of a **zygote** from two **gametes**. Complete the table below.

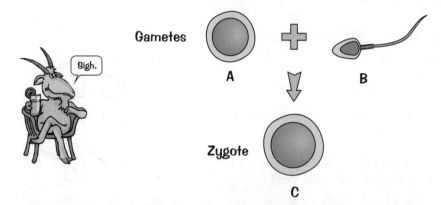

Gametes

A        B

Zygote

C

| | What is it? | Number of chromosomes | Formed by |
|---|---|---|---|
| A | egg | 23 | meiosis |
| B | Sperm | 23 | |
| C | fertilised egg cell | 46 | fertilisation |

**Q3** During sexual reproduction, two **gametes** combine to form a new individual.

a) What are gametes? Sex cells
Cells that have devided by meiosis

b) Explain why gametes have **half** the usual number of chromosomes.
gametes have only one copy of each chromosomes

**Top Tips:** I've tried for ages to come up with a good way of remembering which is mitosis and which is meiosis. Unfortunately I got stuck at "My toes(ies) grow(sies)...", which is rather lame if I may say so myself. I hope for your sake you come up with something better. Good luck...

# Animal Development

**Q1** Use the words provided to complete the passage below.

~~stem cells~~   ~~embryo~~   eight
~~meiosis~~   ~~specialised~~   ~~tissues~~   mitosis

Once an egg is fertilised it divides by ......*Meiosis*...... and forms an ......*embryo*......, made up of embryonic ......*stem cells*...... . These cells can divide to produce any type of ......*specialised*...... cell. After the ......*eight*...... cell stage the cells form ......*tissues*...... and organs.

**Q2** Some **stem cells** are extracted from a **cloned** embryo. Number the stages in the correct order to show how a cloned embryo is produced. The first one has been done for you.

...**1**... Take an egg cell.

...**5**... An embryo forms.

...**3**... Insert the nucleus from a body cell of an adult you want to clone.

...**2**... Remove the genetic material.

...**4**... The inactive genes in the body cell's nucleus are switched on under the right conditions.

...**6**... Extract embryonic stem cells.

**Q3** Describe how **stem cells** are currently used in **medicine**.

*They are used to make organs / ~~cell~~ cure disease*

**Q4** How are **embryonic** stem cells different from **adult** stem cells?

*embronic is extracted from a early stage as Adult Stem cells is at a later stage*

# Plant Development

**Q1**    Plants can produce cells which are **unspecialised**.

a)    Circle the name of the **plant tissue** that produces unspecialised cells.

auxins          mericells          cuttings          meristems

b)    Tick the boxes to show whether the following statements are **true** or **false**.

| | True | False |
|---|---|---|

i)    The plant tissue that produces unspecialised cells can be found in roots and shoots.

ii)    As the plant ages the unspecialised cells lose their ability to become any type of cell. ☑ (False)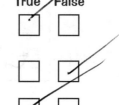

iii)   Any kind of plant cell can be made by the unspecialised cells. ☑ (True)

c)    Give two examples of **tissue** that unspecialised plant cells can form.

1. ........Xylem........          2. ......pholem......

**Q2**    Barry is investigating the effect of rooting powder which contains **plant hormones** on the growth of the roots in some **identical plant cuttings**. His measurements are shown in the table.

a)    What are plant cuttings? ..part of a plant that has been cut off..

b)    Suggest the name of the plant hormones in the rooting powder. auxin

The table shows the effect of the plant hormones concentration on root growth over a week.

| Concentration of plant hormones (parts per million) | 0 | 0.001 | 0.01 | 0.1 | 1 |
|---|---|---|---|---|---|
| Increase in root length (mm) | 6 | 12 | 8 | 3 | 1 |

c)    Plot a **bar chart** below of the increase in root length against the concentration of plant hormones.

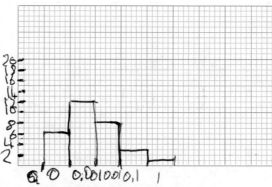

d)    What do the results suggest is the **best concentration** of plant hormones to encourage growth?

......0.001......

---

**Top Tips:**    You often hear about athletes being caught by random drugs tests for using hormones to beef themselves up a bit — I've never heard of any gardeners having their prize vegetable carted off for a random plant hormone test though. Hmmmm...

# Phototropism and Auxins

**Q1**    **Phototropism** is necessary for the survival of plants.

**a)** Explain what **positive** and **negative** phototropism are.

*Positive is (plants need sunlight) - shoots, negitive is roots (grow away from light)*

**b)** Explain why positive and negative phototropism is needed for a plant to **survive**.

Positive phototropism: *Sunlight is needed for Photosynthesis*

Negative phototropism: *nutrients and water is needed for healthy growth.*

**Q2**    Three **plant shoots** (A, B and C) were exposed to a **light stimulus**.
The diagram shows the shape of each shoot before and after the experiment.

**a)** Which part of the plant shoot is **most sensitive** to light?

.........................................

**b)** Which plant **hormones** control growth near this part?

*Auxin*

**c)** On **each** shoot in the diagram, shade in the region that contains the **most** of this hormone.

The black cap and sleeve keep light out.

**Q3**    Two shoot tips were removed from young plants. Agar blocks **soaked in auxins** were placed on the **cut ends** of the **shoots** as shown in the diagram, and they were placed in the dark. The auxins **soak** into the stem where the block touches it.

**a)** Describe the expected responses of shoots A and B to this treatment.

**i)** Shoot A *grow and slant to right*

**ii)** Shoot B *grow straight up/diagonal*

**b)** Explain your answers.

**i)** Shoot A *The left side where the agar jelly block's will cause it to grow more therefore slanting right*

**ii)** Shoot B *The auxin will be speed out easterly therefor all growing at the same rate*

agar jelly blocks

Shoot A   Shoot B

*Module B5 — Growth and Development*

# Mixed Questions — Module B5

**Q1**   Cell division occurs by **meiosis** and **mitosis**.

Draw a line to connect the terms to their descriptions.

| Mitosis... |
| Meiosis... |

...is where cell division produces two new cells that are identical to each other and the parent cell.

...is where cell division produces gametes.

**Q2**   The **bases** in DNA always pair up in the **same** way.

Complete the diagram below to show which **bases** will form the complementary strand of DNA.

| A | C | T | G | C | A | A | T | G |

**Q3**   Number the statements below to show the correct order of the stages involved in making a **protein**.

☐ Amino acids are joined together to make a protein.

☐ Messenger RNA moves out of the nucleus.

☐ A molecule of messenger RNA is made using DNA as a template.

☐ The DNA strand unzips.

☐ Messenger RNA joins with an organelle that makes proteins.

*Organelles are structures inside cells.*

**Q4**   Norbert takes a **cutting** from a part of his ornamental houseplant that contains **meristems**. He's giving the cutting to his aunt so she can grow the plant for herself.

**a)** Explain why it's important for a cutting to contain meristems.

......................................................................................................................

......................................................................................................................

**b)** Circle the correct word to complete the sentences below.

**i)** Plant cuttings can grow into a **seed** / **clone** of the parent plant.

**ii)** Cuttings are usually taken from plants with **desirable** / **unpleasant** features.

**c)** Explain why cuttings are grown with **rooting powder**.

......................................................................................................................

......................................................................................................................

# Mixed Questions — Module B5

**Q5** Some parts of plants grow in response to **light**.

a) Give the name of this response.

......................................................................................................................

b) Decide whether the following statements are **true** or **false**.

True   False

i) Plant shoots grow away from light.

ii) Plant roots grow towards light.

iii) Positive phototropism ensures that roots grow deep into the soil for nutrients.

iv) If the tip of a shoot is removed, the shoot may stop growing.

c) Write the correct version of the **false** statements.

......................................................................................................................

......................................................................................................................

......................................................................................................................

......................................................................................................................

**Q6** Scientists are conducting research into using **embryonic stem cells** to produce tissues and organs.

a) i) What is a **tissue**?

..................................................................................................

ii) What is an **organ**?

..................................................................................................

b) Suggest a reason why some people think it's **unethical** to use embryonic stem cells for research.

......................................................................................................................

......................................................................................................................

c) Circle the correct word from each pair to complete the passage below.

**Some** / **All** of the body cells in an organism contain **the same** / **different** genes and most of the genes are switched **off** / **on**. This is because body cells only need to produce the specific **proteins** / **DNA** they need to function. But in **stem** / **liver** cells any gene can be switched **off** / **on** during their development. The genes that are active determine the **number** / **type** of cells they specialise into.

# Module B6 — Brain and Mind

## The Nervous System

**Q1** Complete the following passage using the words from the box.

| environment | hormonal | change |
|---|---|---|
| receptors | multicellular | nervous |

A stimulus is any ................................... in the ................................... of

an organism, for example a drop in air temperature. Stimuli are detected by

................................... in the ................................... system. This system,

along with the ................................... system, developed as

................................... organisms evolved.

**Q2** The **CNS** makes up part of the **nervous system**.

**a)** What do the letters **CNS** stand for?

......................................................................

**b)** What is the **function** of the CNS?

......................................................................

**c)** On the diagram label the parts that make up the CNS.

**d)** What is the role of the **peripheral** nervous system (PNS)?

......................................................................

......................................................................

**e)** What type of neurones:

**i)** carry information **to** the CNS? ...............................................................

**ii)** carry instructions **from** the CNS? ...............................................................

**Q3** Complete the diagram below to show the pathway of information through the nervous system.

| Stimulus | | | | | | Response |
|---|---|---|---|---|---|---|

# The Nervous System

**Q4**  **Receptors** and **effectors** are important cells in the nervous system.

**a)**  What is the role of effectors?

.........................................................................................................................................

**b)**  What are receptors?

.........................................................................................................................................

**c)**  Put the words below into the correct columns in the table to show the different types of effectors and receptors, and the different **organs** they form part of.

taste buds            glands            the eye            muscle cells

hormone secreting cells            the tongue            muscles            light receptor cells

|  | Example | Make up part of... |
|---|---|---|
| **Receptor** | taste buds | the tongue |
| **Effector** |  |  |

**Q5**  Jamie was cooking his mum some tea when he accidentally picked up a **hot** saucepan.  Jamie **instantly** dropped the pan back onto the hob.

Put numbers in the boxes so that the following statements are in the correct order to describe how Jamie's nervous system responded to him picking up the hot pan.  The first one has been done for you.

[ ]  Some of the muscles in Jamie's hand contract, causing him to drop the pan.

[ 1 ]  Temperature receptors in Jamie's hand detect the increase in temperature.

[ ]  Impulses travel along a motor neurone.

[ ]  Impulses travel along a sensory neurone.

[ ]  The information is processed by the spinal cord.

# Neurones and Synapses

**Q1** The diagram below shows a typical **neurone**.

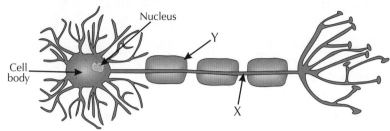

a) How does information travel along the neurone?

.......................................................................................................................................

b) Complete the following sentences by circling the correct word in each pair.

> Structure X is the **synapse** / **axon** of the neurone. It's made from the neurone's
>
> **cytoplasm** / **nucleus** stretched into a long fibre and surrounded by a cell **membrane** / **wall**.

c) Name the part labelled **Y** and describe its function.

.......................................................................................................................................

.......................................................................................................................................

**Q2** The neurones in the body **aren't directly connected** together — there are small **gaps** between them.

a) What **name** is given to the small gap between two neurones?

.......................................................................................................................................

b) Information is transmitted across the gap using **transmitter chemicals**. Explain how this works.

.......................................................................................................................................

.......................................................................................................................................

.......................................................................................................................................

**Q3** Some **drugs** affect **transmission** of impulses around the nervous system.

Describe an effect **ecstasy** (MDMA) has on the synapses in the brain and say why the drug is often described as having 'mood-enhancing effects'.

.......................................................................................................................................

.......................................................................................................................................

.......................................................................................................................................

# Neurones and Synapses

**Q4** Complete the passage below using the words provided.

| blood | fast | effector | slow |
|---|---|---|---|
| oestrogen | chemical | electrical | neurones |

Animals have two types of communication systems. Hormonal communication systems

transmit ................................... signals called hormones (e.g ...................................).

Hormones are carried in the ................................... and tend to cause ................................... ,

long-lasting effects in the body. Nervous communication systems are made up of cells

called ................................... . These cells link receptor cells (e.g. in the eyes) with

................................... cells (e.g. in muscles). Nerve cells carry ...................................

impulses for ................................... , short-lived responses.

**Q5** Brian is depressed. His doctor is considering prescribing Brian **PROZAC®**, so he gives him a leaflet about the drug. Read the passage below and answer the questions that follow.

- PROZAC® is a drug that is sometimes prescribed to people who are suffering from depression.
- PROZAC® works by blocking the sites where the neurotransmitter serotonin is removed.
- This means that the serotonin concentration increases in a person's synapses, which has a mood-enhancing effect.

**a)** PROZAC® and serotonin are both present in the synapses of patients who have taken the drug. Explain why serotonin triggers a **nerve impulse** in neurones, but PROZAC® doesn't.

..............................................................................................................................

..............................................................................................................................

**b)** Name **one** other drug that has the same effect on **serotonin concentration** as PROZAC®.

..............................................................................................................................

**c)** Name **one** other drug that affects the transmission of impulses across synapses.

..............................................................................................................................

**Top Tips:** Hopefully you've got your head around what the nervous system is and how it works. It's really worthwhile making sure you're happy with answering questions on the basics — otherwise you might struggle with some of the topics that pop up later on in the section.

*Module B6 — Brain and Mind*

# _Reflexes_

**Q1** Circle the correct word(s) in each pair to complete the following sentences.

a) Reflexes happen more **quickly** / **slowly** than other responses.

b) The neurones involved in reflexes go through the **back bone** / **spinal cord** or **an unconscious** / **a conscious** part of the brain.

c) Reflexes are **voluntary** / **involuntary**.

d) The nervous pathway of a reflex is called a reflex **arc** / **ellipse**.

e) An impulse always travels along **the same** / **a different** route through a reflex pathway.

**Q2** List three reflexes that **newborn babies** have.

1. ................................................................................................................

2. ................................................................................................................

3. ................................................................................................................

**Q3** **Reflexes** produce many important responses. Tick the boxes below to show whether the following statements are **true** or **false**.

|  | True | False |
|---|---|---|
| a) The pupil reflex focuses light onto the retina to help with vision. | ☐ | ☐ |
| b) Reflex actions help simple animals to respond to some changes in their environment in a way that helps them survive. | ☐ | ☐ |
| c) Reflex actions can help simple animals to find food and hide from predators. | ☐ | ☐ |
| d) Simple animals don't rely entirely on reflexes. | ☐ | ☐ |

**Q4** When you touch something **hot** with a finger you **automatically** pull the finger away. This is an example of a **reflex action**.

Complete the passage using words from the box below.

| motor | sensory | receptors | effector | relay | stimulus | CNS |

When the ............................... is detected by ............................... in the finger an impulse is sent along a ............................... neurone to a ............................... neurone in the ............................... . The impulse is passed to a ............................... neurone, which carries the impulse to the ............................... .

# Modifying and Learning Reflexes

**Q1**  Read the passage about **Pavlov** and answer the questions that follow.

> Pavlov's most famous experiment looked at conditioning in dogs.  The experiment was based on the observation that dogs salivated every time they smelt food.  In his experiment a bell was rung just before the dogs were fed.  Eventually he noticed that the dogs would salivate when the bell was rung even if they couldn't smell food.

**a)**  From the passage, identify the:

  **i)** primary stimulus ......................................................................................................

  **ii)** secondary stimulus ...................................................................................................

  **iii)** unconditioned reflex ...............................................................................................

  **iv)** conditioned reflex ...................................................................................................

**b)**  Which reflex, conditioned or unconditioned, has been learnt?

  ...............................................................................................................

**c)**  Complete the following sentence by circling the correct words.

> In a conditioned reflex the final response has
>
> **a direct connection / no direct connection** to the secondary stimulus.

**Q2**  Birds can **learn** to reject insects with certain colourings — this is a **conditioned reflex**.

**a)**  Put the following statements in order to show how a conditioned reflex can increase a bird's chances of survival.  The first one has been done for you.

  [ ] The bird spots a red coloured caterpillar and avoids it.

  [ ] The bird increases its chances of survival by avoiding the caterpillar and being poisoned.

  [1] A bird spots a red coloured caterpillar.  It swoops down, catches and eats the caterpillar.

  [ ] The bird learns to associate feeling unwell with the red colour.

  [ ] The bird feels unwell because of poisons in the insect.

**b)**  In this example, what is the **primary** stimulus?

  ...............................................................................................................

**Q3**  Give one example of when it would be useful to **modify** a reflex response and describe in terms of neurones how the reflex arc is modified.

  ...............................................................................................................

  ...............................................................................................................

# Brain Development and Learning

**Q1** Tick the boxes to show whether each statement is **true** or **false**.

|  |  | True | False |
|---|---|---|---|
| **a)** | The brain contains around one million neurones. | ☐ | ☐ |
| **b)** | Complex animals with a brain are able to learn by experience. | ☐ | ☐ |
| **c)** | The brain coordinates complex behaviour such as social behaviour. | ☐ | ☐ |
| **d)** | Humans have evolved a smaller brain than other animals, which gives us a survival advantage. | ☐ | ☐ |

**Q2** Complete the passage using words from the box below.

> more      experience      unconnected      network
> stimulated      developed      trillions      formed

Most of the neurone connections in a newborn baby's brain are not yet

........................................, so the brain is only partly ........................................ .

Every new ........................................ causes the brain to become ........................................

developed. When neurones in the brain are ........................................ they branch out,

forming connections between cells that were previously ........................................ .

This forms a massive ........................................ of neurones with ........................................

of different routes for impulses to travel down.

**Q3** Sarah and Sophie both play the **piano**. Sarah has been **practising** all week but Sophie **hasn't practised at all**. The girls' piano teacher, Mr Fudge, compliments Sarah on her performance but tells Sophie that he thinks she needs to practise more next week.

Explain why some skills can be **learnt** through **repetition**.

........................................................................................................................

........................................................................................................................

........................................................................................................................

........................................................................................................................

**Top Tips:**    Hopefully now you'll understand the science behind the phrase 'practice makes perfect'. If that's the case, you should also understand why it's really important to keep going over stuff when you're revising — it's one of the best ways to get stuff stored away in your brain.

# Learning Skills and Behaviour

**Q1** Explain why **complex animals**, such as humans, are able to **adapt** to new situations better than **simple animals**, such as insects.

...........................................................................................................................

...........................................................................................................................

**Q2** Read the two case studies about **feral children** below and answer the questions that follow.

> Isabelle was discovered in 1938 at the age of about six. She'd spent most of her life locked in a darkened room with her mother who was deaf and unable to speak. Isabelle was unable to walk and she had the mental age of a nineteen-month old child. She rapidly learnt to speak and write. By the age of eight Isabelle had reached a 'normal' level and was eventually able to go to school, participating in all activities with other children.

> Eleven-year old Tissa was discovered in 1973 in Sri Lanka. When he was caught he showed many animal characteristics, such as walking on all fours, snarling at humans and yelping. Tissa was taken into care, and although he learned to smile and to eat with his hands, he never learned how to speak.

**a)** Explain why Isabelle couldn't speak when she was discovered.

...........................................................................................................................

**b)** What do the case studies above suggest about language development in children? Use evidence to justify your answer.

...........................................................................................................................

...........................................................................................................................

...........................................................................................................................

**Q3** Hew has been in a **car accident**. Bruising on his **head** suggests that he took a nasty blow during the crash. The doctors are also concerned because he's having difficulty speaking and is unable to remember simple facts.

**a)** What part of Hew's **brain** might have been **damaged**?

...........................................................................................................................

**b)** Name two other things that this part of the brain is important for.

1. .....................................................................................................................

2. .....................................................................................................................

**Top Tips:** Language development isn't the only thing that has to happen before a certain age — balance and hearing also rely on early experiences. It's the same for other animals too — some birds never learn the proper bird song for their species if they're kept in isolation when they're young.

*Module B6 — Brain and Mind*

# _**Studying the Brain**_

**Q1** Studying the brain can be useful for a number of reasons, for example
in the **diagnosis** of people with brain disorders such as Parkinson's disease.
Give **three methods** used by scientists to **map** the regions of the **brain**.

1. .................................................................................................................................

2. .................................................................................................................................

3. .................................................................................................................................

**Q2** What is **memory**?

.................................................................................................................................

**Q3** There are a number of things that can influence how humans remember information.

a) Jerry is trying to remember two phone numbers:

**A. 01951 845217 and B. 01234 543210**

Which number, A or B, is Jerry most likely to remember? Give a reason for your answer.

.................................................................................................................................

.................................................................................................................................

b) If **strong stimuli** are associated with information it can help people to remember it.
Give **three** of these stimuli.

1. .................................... 2. .................................... 3. ....................................

c) Give **one** other method used by humans to make them **more likely** to remember information.

.................................................................................................................................

**Q4 a)** Complete the diagram using the words below to illustrate the **multi-store model** of memory.

**short-term memory      long-term memory      repetition      retrieval      forgotten**

```
                         ┌──────────────┐
                         │              │
                         └──────▲───────┘
┌──────────────┐  ┌──────────┐ │ ┌──────────────┐        ┌──────────────┐
│ information   │──│ attention│→│ │              │────────│              │
└──────────────┘  └──────────┘   └──────▲───────┘  ┌───┐  │              │
                                        │          └───┘  └──────────────┘
                                 ┌──────┴───────┐
                                 │              │
                                 └──────────────┘
```

b) 'The multi-store model offers a complete explanation of how human memory works.'

Is this statement **true** or **false**? .................................................................................

---

_Module B6 — Brain and Mind_

# Mixed Questions — Module B6

**Q1 a)** What is a **stimulus**?

..................................................................................................................................

**b)** Which of the following types of cell can **detect stimuli**? Circle the correct answer.

effectors          receptors

neurones

**c)** What type of cells **receive** impulses from **motor neurones**?

..................................................................................................................................

**d)** Briefly describe the structure and function of the **peripheral nervous system** (PNS).

..................................................................................................................................

..................................................................................................................................

**Q2** Gavin accidentally inhaled some pepper and **sneezed**. A sneeze is an example of a **reflex**.

**a)** Give two other examples of **adult** human reflexes.

1. ...........................................................................................................................

2. ...........................................................................................................................

**b)** Put the following statements in order to describe the path of a reflex arc. The first one has been done for you.

[ ] The impulse is passed along a relay neurone.

[ ] An impulse is sent along a sensory neurone to the CNS.

[ ] The impulse is sent along a motor neurone.

[ ] The impulse reaches an effector, which reacts to the stimulus.

[1] A stimulus is detected by receptor cells.

**c)** Explain why **electrical nerve impulses**, and not **hormones**, are used for reflexes.

..................................................................................................................................

..................................................................................................................................

# Mixed Questions — Module B6

**Q3** The diagram below shows two **nerve cells**.

a) Complete the diagram by adding **labels** in the spaces provided.

i) ...........................................................

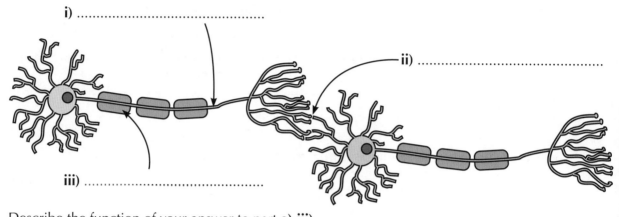

ii) .................................................................

iii) ...............................................................

b) Describe the function of your answer to part **a) iii)**.

..................................................................................................................................................

..................................................................................................................................................

**Q4** Complete the passage using the words below.

| repeated | harder | practised | strengthened | more |
|---|---|---|---|---|

When experiences are ........................................ the pathways that the nerve impulses travel

down become ......................................... . These pathways are ........................................

likely to transmit impulses than others — this makes some activities much easier if you've

......................................... them a lot. After the age of ten, the pathways that aren't used as

often die off. This is why it's ......................................... for older people to learn new things.

**Q5** Stephen picks up his **hot** cup of tea.

a) Describe how the reflex that would normally make Stephen drop the cup can be **modified**.

..................................................................................................................................................

..................................................................................................................................................

b) Explain why it's **useful** for Stephen to modify his reflex response in this situation.

..................................................................................................................................................

# Blood and The Circulatory System

**Q1**  **Blood** is made up of four components.

**a)** Circle the **four** components of blood.

microbes

clear blood cells

red blood cells

plasma

white blood cells

platelets

nucleus

**b)** Tick the boxes to show whether the statements are true or false.

True  False

**i)** The function of red blood cells is to fight germs.

**ii)** White blood cells help to clot blood.

**iii)** Plasma carries waste like carbon dioxide and urea.

**iv)** The liquid part of blood is called urine.

**v)** Platelets help to seal wounds to prevent blood loss.

**vi)** Red blood cells transport oxygen around the body.

**Q2**  Blood carries **substances** around the body.

**a)** Name two substances that blood carries **to** the muscles.

1. ........................................................................................................................

2. ........................................................................................................................

**b)** Name **one** waste product that blood carries **away** from the muscles.

........................................................................................................................

**Q3**  Explain how **red blood cells** are adapted to their function.

........................................................................................................................

........................................................................................................................

........................................................................................................................

........................................................................................................................

# Blood and The Circulatory System

**Q4** The diagram below shows the human **heart**, as seen from the front.
The left atrium has been labelled. Complete the remaining labels a) to e).

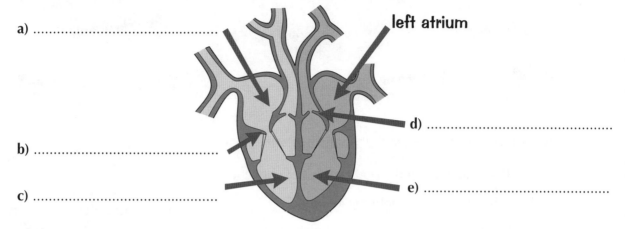

a) .................................................

left atrium

d) ...............................................

b) .................................................

c) .................................................

e) ...............................................

**f)** What is the function of the valves in the heart and in veins?

.......................................................................................................................................

**g)** Use the words given to fill in the blanks in the paragraph below.

| vein | heart | deoxygenated | blood | artery | oxygenated | double |
|------|-------|--------------|-------|--------|------------|--------|

Humans have a ................................... circulatory system. In one circuit,

................................... is pumped from the ................................... to the lungs.

In the other circuit, ................................... blood leaves the heart, is pumped around

the body, and ................................... blood returns to the heart.

**Q5** The diagram shows the **blood vessels** of the **heart**.

**a)** Write the name of each blood vessel beside the letters on the diagram.

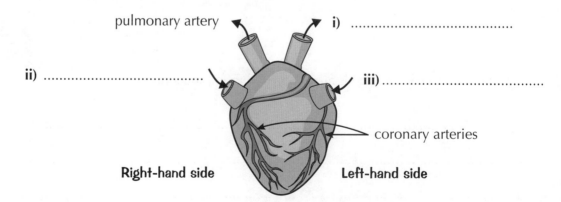

pulmonary artery

i) ......................................

ii) ......................................

iii) ......................................

coronary arteries

Right-hand side

Left-hand side

**b)** What is the function of the coronary arteries?

.......................................................................................................................................

*Module B7 — Further Biology*

# Tissue Fluid and The Skeletal System

**Q1**   **Tissue fluid** surrounds cells.

**a)**   Tick the boxes below to say whether each statement is **true** or **false**.

                                                                        True  False

   **i)**   Capillaries are larger than arteries.                      ☐    ☐

   **ii)**  Capillaries have permeable walls so substances can move in and out easily.   ☐    ☐

   **iii)** Networks of capillaries in tissue are called capillary beds.     ☐    ☐

**b)**   What is the function of tissue fluid?

   ......................................................................................................................................

**c)**   How is tissue fluid formed?

   ..........................................................................................................................

   ......................................................................................................................................

**d)**   **i)**   How do substances move between tissue fluid and cells?

   ......................................................................................................................................

   **ii)**  Name two substances that move from **tissue fluid** into **cells**.

      1. ....................................................................................................................

      2. ....................................................................................................................

   **iii)** Name two substances that move from **cells** into **tissue fluid**.

      1. ....................................................................................................................

      2. ....................................................................................................................

**Q2**   The skeletons of mammals and other **vertebrates** are different from the skeletons of insects.

**a)**   Give one difference between a vertebrate's skeleton and an insect's skeleton.

   ......................................................................................................................................

**b)**   What are the functions of a vertebrate's skeleton?

   ......................................................................................................................................

   ......................................................................................................................................

---

**Top Tips:**   Tissue fluid might not sound as tasty as a nice cup of tea, but it means that your body doesn't need to have mile after mile of capillaries just so your cells can get all the nutrients they need.  Make sure you know what the function of tissue fluid is and how it's formed.

# Tissue Fluid and The Skeletal System

**Q3** **Joints** allow the bones of the skeleton to move.

a) Complete the labels i) to v).

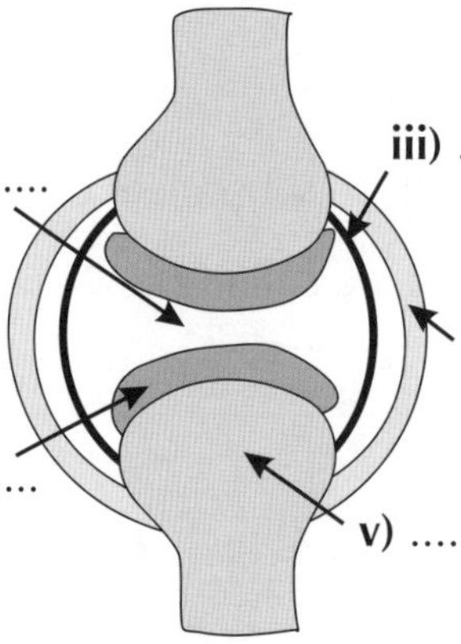

i) ..................................................

iii) ..................................................

iv) ..................................................

ii) ..................................................

v) ..................................................

b) Circle the correct words to complete the following sentences.

> The joint is stabilised by elastic **cartilage / ligaments** which hold the bones together but still allow movement. A smooth layer of **cartilage / ligaments** prevents the **muscles / bones** rubbing together, which reduces friction between them. The synovial **membrane / fluid** is an oily substance which **lubricates / heats** the joint, allowing it to move more easily.

**Q4** **Muscles** often work in **pairs**.

a) In the diagram, which muscle is **contracted** and which is **relaxed**? Tick the correct boxes.

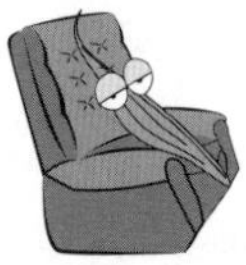

|  | Contracted | Relaxed |
|---|---|---|
| Biceps | ☐ | ☐ |
| Triceps | ☐ | ☐ |

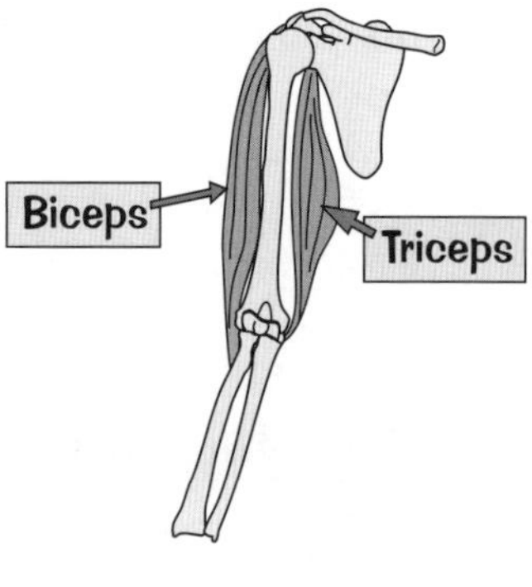

Biceps

Triceps

b) Explain how muscles move bones at joints in the body.

..................................................................................................

..................................................................................................

..................................................................................................

..................................................................................................

..................................................................................................

# Exercise and Fitness

**Q1**     Grania has asked a personal trainer to design a **fitness regime** for her.

**a)**     Circle the useful question(s) the personal trainer may ask Grania.

> Do you have any health problems like high blood pressure?

> How many brothers or sisters do you have?

> Are you taking any medication?

> Do you smoke?

> How many GCSEs do you have?

**b)**     Why might the personal trainer ask Grania about her **family medical history**?

.............................................................................................................................................

**Q2**     Jim and George take part in a 400 metre race.  The **graph** below shows their **heart rates** before, during and after the race.

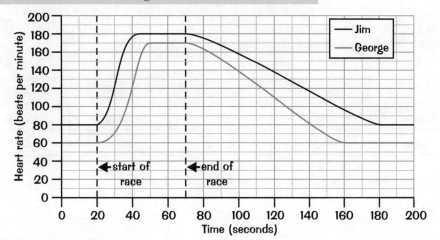

**a)**     Give the **resting** heart rate of:

    **i)** Jim:          .........................................................................................

    **ii)** George:    .......................................................................................

**b)**     Give the **maximum** heart rate of:

    **i)** Jim:          .....................................................................

    **ii)** George:    ...................................................................

**c)**  **i)**  Calculate Jim's **recovery period**.

.............................................................................................................................................

    **ii)** Calculate George's **recovery period**.

.............................................................................................................................................

    **iii)** Which of the two is the **fittest**?  Give one reason for your answer.

.............................................................................................................................................

# Exercise and Fitness

**Q3** Body mass index (**BMI**) can be used as an indicator of a person's fitness.

**a)** Daniel is 1.7 metres tall and weighs 76 kg. Calculate his BMI.

$$BMI = \frac{body\ mass\ in\ kg}{(height\ in\ m)^2}$$

........................................................

........................................................

**b)** Look at the table on the right. What is Daniel's weight description?

........................................................

| Body Mass Index | Weight Description |
|---|---|
| below 18.5 | underweight |
| 18.5 - 24.9 | normal |
| 25 - 29.9 | overweight |
| 30 - 40 | moderately obese |
| above 40 | severely obese |

**Q4** Tanya and Kara have been following an exercise regime. They've been monitoring their **progress** by recording changes in their **proportion of body fat**. Their results are shown in the table below.

| | January | February | March | April | May |
|---|---|---|---|---|---|
| Tanya | 29% | 27% | 25% | 24% | 23% |
| Kara | 35% | 32% | 30% | 28% | 26% |

**a) i)** Who out of Tanya and Kara was the most fit in January?

........................................................

**ii)** Who out of Tanya and Kara showed the greatest change in fitness between January and May?

........................................................

**b)** Kara thinks the data she's recorded isn't **accurate**. Her fitness instructor suggests she checks the **repeatability** of her monitoring procedure. Write a brief explanation of the terms accuracy and repeatability.

**i)** Accuracy

........................................................

........................................................

**ii)** Repeatability

........................................................

........................................................

*Module B7 — Further Biology*

# Exercise and Injury

**Q1**     **Excessive exercise** can cause **injuries**.

    **a)**    Draw lines to connect the type of injury to its correct description.

        Sprain     a bone comes out a socket.

        Dislocation     damage to a ligament, usually caused by being stretched too much.

    **b)**    Give two other examples of injuries from excessive exercise.

      1. ....................................................................................................................................

      2. ....................................................................................................................................

**Q2**     Some injuries caused by excessive exercise may require **special care**.

      Circle the correct word(s) from each pair to complete the following paragraph.

> More serious injuries may be treated by a **physiotherapist** / **psychologist**,
>
> who specialises in injuries of the **cardiovascular** / **skeletal-muscular** system.
>
> They will **give treatment** / **do surgery** to reduce swelling and pain, and
>
> give therapies to **slow down** / **speed up** healing. They will also advise
>
> on the best **clothing** / **exercises** to help **rehabilitate** / **cure** the affected area.

**Q3 a)**    List the two main **symptoms** of a **sprain**.

      1. ...........................................................................

      2. ...........................................................................

    **b)**    Describe a basic treatment for a sprained ankle.

      ....................................................................................................................................

      ....................................................................................................................................

      ....................................................................................................................................

      ....................................................................................................................................

      ....................................................................................................................................

# Controlling Body Temperature

**Q1**   The human body is usually maintained at a temperature of about **37 ºC**.

**a)**   Circle the correct word to complete the following sentence.

To maintain a constant temperature, the heat gained by the body

is **balanced by** / **greater than** the heat lost by the body.

**b)**   **i)**   Name the part of the **brain** that detects the temperature of the **blood**.

..................................................................................................................................

**ii)**   Describe **one** other role of the part of the brain named above in controlling body temperature.

..................................................................................................................................

..................................................................................................................................

**c)**   Name the location in the body of temperature receptors that monitor the **external** temperature.

..................................................................................................................................

**Q2**   **Receptors** and **effectors** regulate body temperature.

**a)**   What is the name of the **mechanism** that enables the body to keep its temperature constant?

..................................................................................................

*'Homeostasis' isn't the answer to this one.*

**b)**   **i)**   Describe the role of a **receptor** in regulating body temperature.

..................................................................................................................................

**ii)**   Describe the role of an **effector** in regulating body temperature.

..................................................................................................................................

**iii)** Name two **effectors** involved in the regulation of body temperature.

1. ..............................................................................................................................

2. ..............................................................................................................................

**c)**   Why do some effectors work **antagonistically**?

..................................................................................................................................

..................................................................................................................................

---

**Top Tips:**   Some animals don't have such a fancy homeostatic system to control temperature. Some reptiles have to bask in sunlight until their blood has warmed up before they can go about their business.  I wouldn't mind lounging around in the sun for a couple of hours before work every day...

# *Controlling Body Temperature*

**Q3** The body has a number of **mechanisms** to control its temperature.

a) Which of these diagrams illustrates the skin's response to **hot** temperatures?
Explain your answer.

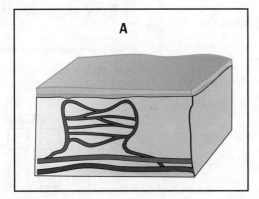

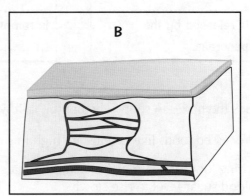

Diagram .......... because ........................................................................................................

.............................................................................................................................................

.............................................................................................................................................

b) Give **one** other process that can help the body to **cool down** when it's too hot.

.............................................................................................................................................

**Q4** Complete the passage using some of the words provided below.

| cold | dehydrated | hot | exercising |
|------|------------|-----|------------|
| increase | evaporates | decrease | |

When you're too ............................................... you produce a lot of sweat, and

when it ............................................... it uses heat and cools your body. But if you

sweat too much when you're ............................................... then the water loss can

make you ............................................... . This means you'll produce far less sweat

so your core body temperature will ............................................... .

**Q5** Shivering can help the body to **warm up** when it's too cold.

a) Which parts of the body are the **effectors** in shivering?

.............................................................................................................................................

b) Explain how shivering helps to increase body temperature.

.............................................................................................................................................

.............................................................................................................................................

*Module B7 — Further Biology*

# Controlling Blood Sugar

**Q1**    Complete the flow chart to show what happens
when the level of sugar in the blood gets **too high**.

| ............................... is released by the pancreas. | → | ............................... is removed from the ................................ . | → | Blood sugar level is now ................................ . |
|---|---|---|---|---|

**Q2**    Tick the boxes to show whether the following statements are **true** or **false**.

**True   False**

a)  Processed foods like cereals are high in simple sugars.           ☐  ☐

b)  Eating foods that are high in simple sugars causes your
blood sugar level to rise slowly.                                     ☐  ☐

c)  Simple sugars are digested and absorbed into the blood very slowly.   ☐  ☐

d)  Blood sugar level is controlled by a hormone called insulin.      ☐  ☐

**Q3**    **Diabetes** is where blood sugar level can't be controlled properly.

a)  i)  What is **type 1** diabetes?

    .................................................................................................................

    ii) How is type 1 diabetes **controlled**?

    .................................................................................................................

b)  i)  What is **type 2** diabetes?

    .................................................................................................................

    ii) Suggest two things that **increase** your **risk** of developing type 2 diabetes.

        1. ............................................................    2. ............................................................

    iii) Suggest two ways of **controlling** type 2 diabetes.

        1. ............................................................    2. ............................................................

**Q4**    Compared to a diet high in simple sugars, explain how a diet high in **fibre**
and **complex carbohydrates** helps to maintain a constant blood sugar level.

.................................................................................................................

.................................................................................................................

.................................................................................................................

# The Industrial Use of Microorganisms

**Q1** Microorganisms like fungi and bacteria are used to make products on an industrial scale.

a) Circle the features of microorganisms that make them **useful** for industrial production methods.

> They can make complex molecules.

> They have plasmids.

> They never have a bad hair day.

> They can cause disease.

> They're not aggressive.

> They reproduce rapidly.

b) Suggest two other reasons why microorganisms are used to make products on a large scale.

1. ......................................................................................................

2. ......................................................................................................

**Q2** Describe how microorganisms are used to produce **one** type of **biofuel**.

......................................................................................................

......................................................................................................

**Q3** Microorganisms are used to make many different **products**.

a) Name a **medicine** that's produced on a large scale using microorganisms.

......................................................................................................

b) Describe how microorganisms are involved in the production of **washing powder**.

......................................................................................................

c) i) Describe how microorganisms are involved in the production of **vegetarian cheese**.

......................................................................................................

......................................................................................................

......................................................................................................

ii) Name **one** other vegetarian food product that's made using microorganisms.

......................................................................................................

**Top Tips:** We can produce huge amounts of products by growing microorganisms in containers called fermenters. Fermenters are kept at the optimum conditions for growth so the microorganisms will produce the biggest possible amount of the products we want. Hurrah.

*Module B7 — Further Biology*

# Genetic Modification

**Q1**  **Genetic modification** is a technique that has many useful applications.

Circle the correct definition of genetic modification.

> Genetic modification is where all the cells in an organism are duplicated.

> Genetic modification is where the cytoplasm in an organism is replaced.

> Genetic modification is where a gene from one organism is transferred to another.

**Q2**  One **application** of genetic modification is medicine production.

**a)**  Name **one** medicine that's made by a genetically modified organism.

............................................................................................................................................

**b)**  Give **one** other application of genetic modification.

............................................................................................................................................

**Q3**  **Genetic modification** can be used to change organisms to make them more useful.

**a)**  Put these stages of genetic modification in order by numbering them 1–4.

☐ Vectors containing the gene are transferred into new cells.

☐ The gene is isolated and replicated.

☐ Each gene is joined to a vector.

☐ The modified cells are selected.

*The ultimate in genetic modification.*

**b)**  Name **two** types of vectors.

1. ......................................................................................................................................

2. ......................................................................................................................................

**c)**  Why can genes from one organism be transferred into another organism and continue to work?

............................................................................................................................................

# *Biological Technologies*

**Q1**    **Genetic testing** can be used to identify **genetic disorders**.

a)   Circle the type of cell that DNA is usually taken from for genetic testing.

red blood cells

pancreas cells

skin cells

white blood cells

liver cells

b)   **Gene probes** are often used in genetic testing.

**i)** What is a gene probe?

......................................................................................................................................................

**ii)** How do gene probes locate a specific gene?

......................................................................................................................................................

c)   Number the boxes (1-5) to show how a gene probe is used to identify a faulty gene.

☐   The chemical marker is located on the DNA.

☐   The gene probe is mixed with DNA.

☐   A gene probe is produced with a chemical marker attached.

☐   The gene probe sticks to the gene.

☐    A DNA sample is taken.

> Gene
> Probe
> Private
> Detective

**Q2**    **Fluorescent chemical markers** are used to **locate** gene probes.

a)   How can a fluorescent chemical marker be used to locate a gene probe?

......................................................................................................................................................

b)   Suggest two pieces of information a gene probe with a marker tells you about a DNA sample.

1. ................................................................................................................................................

2. ................................................................................................................................................

---

**Top Tips:**    Technology is moving fast, so the techniques used to test for genetic disorders are continually improving.  Genetic testing sounds great, but like with lots of things these days it comes with a whole host of social and ethical issues... which you should've covered way back in Module B1.

# Biological Technologies

**Q3 a)** What is **biomedical engineering**?

......................................................................................................................................

**b)** Complete the passage using the words provided. Each may be used more than once or not at all.

| | | | |
|---|---|---|---|
| faulty | beats | animal | irregular |
| pacemaker | valves | regular | mechanical |

The heart has a group of cells that determines how fast it ............................ .

Sometimes, these cells stop working properly, and the heartbeat becomes

............................ . In this case, an artificial ............................ is fitted.

............................ heart valves can also be replaced either with

............................ or ............................ valves.

**Q4** **Nanotechnology** can improve the packaging of food products.

**a)** Circle the correct word to complete the sentence below.

Nanotechnology uses structures that are about the same size as **molecules / cells**.

The hippest Grans have all
the latest in nana-technology.

**b)** Suggest two advantages of using nanotechnology in the **packaging** of food products.
Give an **example** for each advantage you mention.

1. ..............................................................................................................................

......................................................................................................................................

2. ..............................................................................................................................

......................................................................................................................................

**Q5** Illnesses can be treated using **stem cell technology**.

**a)** Describe **one** way that stem cells are currently used to treat illnesses.

......................................................................................................................................

......................................................................................................................................

......................................................................................................................................

......................................................................................................................................

**b)** Describe **one** way that stem cells could be used to treat illnesses in the future.

......................................................................................................................................

*Module B7 — Further Biology*

# Ecosystems

**Q1** Ecosystems are a type of **closed loop system**.

**a)** Tick the box next to the correct description of a **perfect closed loop system**.

The outputs from processes and stores within the system are lost as waste. ☐

The outputs from processes and stores within the system are used as inputs to other processes and stores in the system so there's no waste. ☐

Nearly all the inputs to the system come from outside of the system. ☐

**b)** Give **one** reason why ecosystems are **not** perfect closed loop systems.
Use an example in your answer.

...................................................................................................................................................

...................................................................................................................................................

**Q2** Fill in the missing words to complete the sentences below.
The words can be used more than once.

| photosynthesis | reactant | waste product | respiration |

Plants make oxygen as a ................................... during ................................... . Oxygen is used

as a ................................... by plants, animals and microorganisms during ................................... .

Carbon dioxide is produced during ................................... as a ...................................

— it's used by plants as a ................................... during ................................... .

**Q3** Some organisms in ecosystems produce large numbers of **reproductive structures**.

**a)** Give three examples of a reproductive structure.

1. ...............................................................................................................................................

2. ...............................................................................................................................................

3. ...............................................................................................................................................

**b)** Why do some organisms produce lots of reproductive structures?

...................................................................................................................................................

**c)** Is the production of large numbers of reproductive structures **wasteful**? Explain your answer.

...................................................................................................................................................

...................................................................................................................................................

...................................................................................................................................................

*Module B7 — Further Biology*

# *Ecosystems*

**Q4**    The diagram below shows the amount of **water** that goes **in and out** of the Ziglian Rainforest (on the planet Zog) per day.

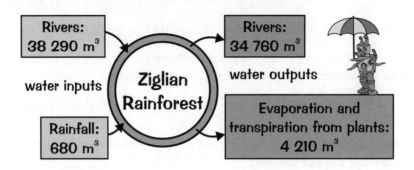

In terms of water, is the Ziglian Rainforest a **stable** ecosystem?  Explain your answer.

.................................................................................................................................................

.................................................................................................................................................

**Q5**    Read the passage below and answer the following questions.

> Removing vegetation can have many consequences, as the people
> who live in the Leafleaf Rainforest have discovered.  After a huge
> number of trees were cleared from the rainforest to create more
> land for crops, the rate of soil erosion increased dramatically.
> This has caused problems for the inhabitants of Leafleaf,
> such as increased flooding from the silting of rivers.

**a)**   **i)**  What is **soil erosion**?

.................................................................................................................................................

**ii)** Use your **own knowledge** to explain why removing
vegetation from the rainforest increased soil erosion.

.................................................................................................................................................

.................................................................................................................................................

........................................................................................

*You'll need to think outside
the box for these questions
and apply what you've learnt
in a slightly different way.*

**b)**   Suggest two impacts other than increased soil erosion
that removing vegetation can have.

1. ...........................................................................................................................................

2. ...........................................................................................................................................

# Human Impacts On Ecosystems

**Q1**  Human activities can unbalance natural ecosystems by **changing inputs** and **outputs**.

**a)  i)** Circle the following activities which **unbalance** natural ecosystems.

| over-fishing | using sunlight energy | flying a kite |

| planting a new tree for every tree cut down | unsustainable timber harvesting |

**ii)** Describe how **one** of the activities you circled unbalances natural ecosystems.

...................................................................................................................................

**b)** Clearing vegetation for **livestock** and **growing crops** can also unbalance ecosystems. Describe two effects of these activities.

1. ..............................................................................................................................

...................................................................................................................................

2. ..............................................................................................................................

...................................................................................................................................

**Q2**  Human systems that use **fossil fuels** are **not** closed loop systems.

**a)** Complete the passage using some of the words provided below.

| old | crude oil | waste emissions |
| outside | the moon | within | the Sun |

Many human systems use fossil fuels like ...................................... as a source of energy.

However, using fossil fuels prevents these systems from being closed loop systems for

many reasons. For example, when they're used they produce ......................................

that aren't used again in the system. Using fossil fuels inputs energy into the system from

...................................... of it, as it comes from ...................................... millions of years

ago. Because fossil fuels take millions of years to form, they can't be made again

...................................... the system.

**b)** Suggest another reason why human systems aren't closed loops.

...................................................................................................................................

> **Top Tips:**  Ecosystems might not be as cute and cuddly as polar bears, but they need protecting. We rely on ecosystems for pretty much everything, from the food we eat to the air we breathe — so it's pretty crazy that we do so much damage to them.

*Module B7 — Further Biology*

# Human Impacts On Ecosystems

**Q3** The diagram below shows a **food chain** based around a stream. It's been polluted by mercury — a heavy metal and a type of **non-recyclable waste**.

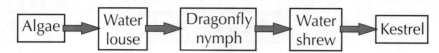

Algae → Water louse → Dragonfly nymph → Water shrew → Kestrel

a) Which of the organisms in the food chain is **most likely** to suffer because of the pollution?

.......................................................................................................................................

b) Explain your answer to part **a)**.

.......................................................................................................................................

.......................................................................................................................................

**Q4** Carla measured the concentration of **nitrates** and the average number of fish per cubic meter of water in the River Numbscull between 2002 and 2010. Her results are shown in the table below.

| | 2002 | 2004 | 2006 | 2008 | 2010 |
|---|---|---|---|---|---|
| Nitrate concentration (milligrams per litre) | 22 | 33 | 48 | 63 | 74 |
| Average number of fish per cubic metre of water | 23 | 21 | 10 | 1 | 0 |

a) i) Describe the change in the concentration of **nitrates** in the river between 2002 and 2010.

.......................................................................................................................................

ii) Describe the change in the average number of **fish** per cubic metre of water in the river between 2002 and 2010.

.......................................................................................................................................

b) i) Give the name of the process that is illustrated by the data in the table.

.......................................................................................................................................

ii) Explain how this process caused the change in the average number of fish per cubic metre of water.

.......................................................................................................................................

.......................................................................................................................................

.......................................................................................................................................

.......................................................................................................................................

.......................................................................................................................................

# Managing Ecosystems

**Q1**  Humans rely on ecosystems for many things.

Tick the correct boxes to show whether the following are **true** or **false**.

**True  False**

a)  Ecosystems provide humans with water.

b)  Pollination is where pollen grains pollute rivers.

c)  Crop production needs pollination.

d)  Ecosystems provide humans with clean air.

e)  Ecosystems provide humans with fertile soil for crop growth.

f)  Fertile soil lacks mineral nutrients.

g)  Ecosystems provide humans with food like game and fish.

**Q2**  There are many ways that resources can be used **sustainably**.

a)  Give a definition of **sustainability**.

......................................................................................................................................

......................................................................................................................................

b)  Describe how **fishing** and **timber harvesting** have changed to become more sustainable.

i)  Fishing:

......................................................................................................................................

ii) Timber harvesting:

......................................................................................................................................

**Q3**  **Sunlight** is a sustainable source of energy.

a)  Why is sunlight a sustainable source of energy?

......................................................................................................................................

b)  Explain how sunlight is used as a sustainable source of energy for:

i)  natural ecosystems.

......................................................................................................................................

......................................................................................................................................

ii) sustainable agriculture.

......................................................................................................................................

......................................................................................................................................

# Mixed Questions — Module B7

**Q1**  Draw lines to the connect the following features of **joints** to their functions.

tendons      lubricates joints

synovial fluid      reduces friction between bones

elastic ligaments      stabilise joints while allowing movement

smooth layer of cartilage      transmit forces from muscles to bones

**Q2**  **Leukaemia** is an illness that has a variety of symptoms, including anaemia — a reduction in the number of **red blood cells** a person has.

**a)**  Circle the features of red blood cells.

pancake shape      packed full of clotting agents      biconcave shape

packed full of haemoglobin      no nucleus      large nucleus

**b)**  Describe how leukaemia can be treated.

..............................................................................................................................................

..............................................................................................................................................

**Q3**  The **heart** beats at a certain rate to pump blood around the body.

right atrium    left atrium

right ventricle    left ventricle

**a)**  The diagram on the left shows the chambers of the heart. Which chamber:

**i)**  Receives blood from the body? ...........................................

**ii)** Pumps blood to the lungs?     ...........................................

**iii)** Receives blood from the lungs? ...........................................

**iv)** Pumps blood to the body?     ...........................................

**b)**  The cells that determine how fast the heart beats can stop working properly. Describe how **biomedical engineering** has been used to fix this problem.

..............................................................................................................................................

..............................................................................................................................................

**Q4**  Explain why trying to protect natural ecosystems can cause **tensions** in some communities.

..............................................................................................................................................

..............................................................................................................................................

*Module B7 — Further Biology*